Second Edition

50
fun ways
→ to
internet

By
Allan Hoffman

CAREER PRESS
3 Tice Road, P.O. Box 687
Franklin Lakes, NJ 07417
1-800-CAREER-1
201-848-0310 (NJ and outside U.S.)
FAX: 201-848-1727

50 FUN WAYS TO INTERNET, 2ND ED.

ISBN 1-56414-342-2, $12.99

Cover design by The Visual Group

Printed in the U.S.A. by Book-mart Press

To order this title by mail, please include price as noted above, $2.50 handling per order, and $1.50 for each book ordered. Send to: Career Press, Inc., 3 Tice Road, P.O. Box 687, Franklin Lakes, NJ 07417.

Or call toll-free 1-800-CAREER-1 (in NJ and Canada: 201-848-0310) to order using VISA or MasterCard, or for further information on books from Career Press.

Library of Congress Cataloging-in-Publication Data

Hoffman, Allan, 1962-
    50 fun ways to Internet / by Allan Hoffman.--2nd ed.
      p.   cm.
    Includes index.
    ISBN 1-56414-342-2 (pbk.)
    1. Internet (Computer network).   I. Title
TK5105.875.I57H63   1998
025.04--dc21
                                      97-49096
                                        CIP

Acknowledgments

I would like to thank my brother, Dan Hoffman, who offered valuable suggestions at the early stages of writing this book, and Stephanie Grant and Matt Goldstein, for their advice and encouragement of my work.

And, always, my parents, Ruth and Sam Hoffman.

Contents

Introduction   9

10 Frequently Asked Questions About the Net   11

Conventions   15

How to Use This Book   17

Part I: Navigating the Net

1. Lost in Cyberspace   23
2. Write to the Prez   26
3. Chat, Chat, Chat   28
4. Lurking and Posting   31
5. Future Forecast   36
6. The Net Intelligentsia   39
7. Build Your Own Home   43
8. Push Me!   45
9. Plugged In   48
10. Search, and Ye Shall Find   52

Part II: Cruising the Net

11. The Art of the Flame   61
12. Netiquette   65
13. The Virtual World   68
14. Search for a Long-Lost Friend   76
15. Networking Party   81
16. Finding a FAQ!   83
17. Love, Cyberstyle   85
18. Celebs of Cyberspace   89
19. Use a :-)   91
20. Not for Women Only   94
21. An Answer for Every Question   96
22. Going Once, Going Twice   99
23. School Days   101
24. Zineworld   105
25. Deep in the Heart of MUDville   107

26. You Don't Know What? 110
27. Stopping by the Software Storehouse 113
28. The Classics, Online 116
29. Your Own Arcade! 118
30. All the Jargon That's Fit to Print 121
31. On the Road 124
32. Surfing the City 128
33. The Museum, Via Your Mouse 130
34. Your John Hancock 132
35. The White House, Online 135
36. Author, Author 138
37. Write to a Letter-Writer 140
38. Chat With the Stars 142
39. Dr. Internet 146
40. Your Song 149
41. Your Ancestors, Online 151

42. Of Neiman Marcus Cookies and   156
     Other Urban Legends

43. Buy, Buy, Buy   158

44. Hot and Wired for the New Millennium   161

45. Your Chat Companions   163

46. In the Land of the FurryMUCKers   170

47. Gender Bending   173

48. Searching by Subject   175

49. Be an Expert   178

50. Explore!   180

    Glossary   181

    Index   185

Introduction

Attempting to navigate the Internet for the first time can be an overwhelming experience. There's a certain exhilaration in being on the Net, but then most people ask themselves a question: Where do I go from here? It's something like arriving in New York City for the first time with nothing but a subway map and a list of vague suggestions from friends, like "visit the Theater District" and "explore Greenwich Village." You know it's an amazing place, but where do you start? You don't want to stand at the corner of Fifth Avenue and 42nd Street all day with a vacant stare, feeling like a yokel among the masses. You've arrived, you're ready to explore, but what now?

Perhaps you've found yourself in a similar position when you've connected to the Net. Maybe you've got a jargon-filled manual with a few addresses of sites on the Net, but you want more detailed information on potential destinations. The culture of the Internet is astonishingly diverse, with everything from pedantic discussions of Wittgenstein to games known as MUDS (Multi-User Dungeons). But it's not all that easy to gain access to the Net's diverse offerings; even experienced users often haven't explored some of the most interesting sites. You want something other than an intimidating book full of commands you'll probably never use. You need a tourist's guide, with suggested destinations and information on how to get to those spots and what you'll find.

Well, here it is.

50 Fun Ways to Internet is a simple guide to exploring the Internet's most interesting sites. As with the Internet itself, much has changed in this second edition. Readers of the first edition will find scores of new sites and a greater emphasis on the resources available on the World Wide Web. The book continues to highlight the diversity of activities and information available in Netland, ranging from Dante criticism to dictionaries, from role-playing games, to chats with celebrities. Written in a conversational style, it's a book for both new users, known as "newbies" on the Net, and more experienced denizens of Netland seeking ideas for further exploration. *50 Fun Ways to Internet* eschews the technical jargon and focuses on what most people want to know: What can I do on the Net?

In the following pages, you will learn about 50 of the Net's most exciting and unique sites, activities and resources. You will participate in a cyberspace auction, wander around the campus of an online university and look at Renaissance art in an exhibit at the Louvre. The Net can be a wild and raucous place, and sometimes you may not like what you read or see; if the indecorous personal ads or the contents of some discussion groups offend you, feel free to skip them. No matter what your interests, you're likely to find something new and exciting in the uncharted terrain of the electronic frontier.

10 Frequently Asked Questions About the Net

1. What is the Internet?

The Internet is a network of thousands and thousands of computers connected around the world. The Internet links not only computers, but *networks* of computers—it's a network of networks, making it possible for people at schools, private companies and other organizations, as well as in their homes, to communicate with each other. Developed as an experimental military network, the Internet has been around for about 25 years, expanding in the 1970s and 80s to serve researchers and educators eager to share ideas and information.

Now, as we're at the end of the millennium, the Internet has become a way for folks of all kinds—sci-fi freaks, entrepreneurs, aficionados of antiques—to talk to each other, play games, conduct business and even buy things. If a friend tells you he's "on the Net," he's probably talking about the Internet, the world's largest computer network.

2. What equipment do I need to connect to the Internet?

You need a personal computer and a modem. There's no need to spend big bucks on a new PC, but if you want to access some of the most exciting features of the Internet—those allowing you to view photographs and video—you'll want a speedy computer with a color monitor and audio capabilities. (In the world of computers, of course, what's speedy one month may be slow the next.)

A modem allows your computer to talk to other computers over telephone lines. It converts the digital signals of your computer into the analog signals used by phones. The faster a modem does that, the better. You can buy a 28,800 bps (bits per second) modem for less than $100.

3. What software do I need?

You need a package of software to manage the connection between your computer, your modem and the remote computer of your Internet service provider. Most service providers include the necessary software when you sign up.

4. How do I get an Internet connection?

Most individual users connect through a national service provider, such as America Online, or a local provider. Others connect through an area college or through work. If you're not a student, consider a local provider or a national online service. For many people, a local access provider will be the best option; if you're near a city, it's likely there's one offering connections at a reasonable price. To find out about local access providers, call your library or a computer store—they'll know about the best ones in your area. For national providers, see the list under question #6.

---

5. How much does it cost to connect to the Internet?

A monthly charge of $19.95 is considered the standard price for unlimited Internet access.

6. What's the difference between the Internet and commercial online services such as America Online and CompuServe?

The Internet is a decentralized, noncommercial network; once you're on the Internet, just about everything, aside from something you want to buy, like a book or flowers, is free. Commercial services offer access to resources not available on the Internet, such as specific games and publications. You can contact them at the following numbers:

America Online	800-827-6364
CompuServe	800-848-8199
Microsoft Network	800-373-3676
Prodigy	800-PRODIGY

7. Who owns the Internet?

No one, really. There's no grand pooh-bah of the Internet. It's not a profit-making venture. Each of the thousands of networks linked together to form the Internet has control of its own domain. A university, for instance, can decide what resources on its computer network to make available to Internet users.

8. What can I do on the Internet?

You can talk to other people, retrieve and look at works of art, access an assortment of reference books...the list is endless, and always growing. Each day, the Net's offerings increase in diversity. Now you can read magazines on the Net, buy flowers and conduct discussions of dreams or disabilities. Check out an online publication like HotWired

(Chapter 44) to get a sense of where the Net is headed; the publication combines text, images and video with "a community space" for discussion among HotWired contributors and readers.

9. How do I get around the Internet?

You can use a variety of tools and programs to get around the Net. E-mail is the easiest—you send a message to someone else and, within a few seconds, that person receives the message. Other methods of getting around the Net include "push technology" and the World Wide Web. The first part of this book, *Navigating the Net*, explains the most common methods of Internet travel.

10. What happens if I get lost on the Internet?

You sink into a dark void. Thousands of netnauts have been lost forever, never to return, their friends posting plaintive messages and photographs to the **alt.have.you.seen.me** newsgroup.

Just kidding. Really, there's nothing wrong with getting lost on the Internet. Calm down, look around, and you might find something interesting on the outer edges of Netland.

Conventions

The following conventions will be used in the book:

Internet and e-mail addresses will be in bold (i.e., **http://www.web100.com**, **alt.sex** and **blaze@well.com**).

Information to be entered as part of an Internet search will be in bold (i.e., **+springsteen +badlands**).

"Placeholders" (items to be completed by the reader) will be italicized (i.e., *your_email_address*).

Within examples, instructions typed by the reader will be in bold (i.e., **open door**).

How to Use
This Book

If you're like most people, you don't want to read a book with pages and pages of arcane computer jargon. Read a book like that, and your eyes turn bleary before you've even typed a few commands on the keyboard. You want to do things, like buy a CD or chat with a stranger in Denmark, rather than read theoretical examples of how to do them.

From the start, this book focuses on fun and useful things to do on the Net. It doesn't waste time with dull techno-babble and esoteric instructions. Like the title says, it's a book for people who want to do fun things on the Internet.

Different people have different ways of approaching a book like this one. Some of you, especially those familiar with the Net (or possessing a high level of assurance—or recklessness—with computers), will begin to read *50 Fun Ways to Internet* by flipping through it, looking for things of interest—a role-playing game, say, or an online art exhibit. Others will be more cautious, starting at Chapter 1 and moving ahead carefully, chapter by chapter. You can read this book either way, depending on how much you know about the Net, if anything, and how much you're driven to explore. Whatever your approach, note the book's division into *Part I: Navigating the Net* and *Part II: Cruising the Net*. The 10 chapters of *Part I* explain the essentials of Internet travel, while the remaining chapters are written with the assumption that you're familiar with the previously covered essentials.

Newcomers to the Net should start with *Part I: Navigating the Net*. This section guides you through the basic skills for surfing cyberspace. Trying out activities such as building a home page or writing to the president will help you gain a basic familiarity with the Net and how to get around it. If you're already a nethead, there's no need to start with *Part I*, but don't ignore the first 10 chapters. Reading them, you're likely to learn about sites you haven't encountered.

Once you start skipping around the book, as you're likely to do (it's meant for that!), just remember that if you get stuck—if you're not sure how to use "plug-ins" or "push technology" or any of the other programs and tools discussed here—you can always return to the first 10 chapters to find out what to do. Let's say you're reading about Shockwave games discussed in Chapter 29, but you can't remember the details of using the Shockwave plug-in. What do you do? Flip back to Chapter 9, where plug-ins are explained, for an answer. Whenever you're stuck, refer to *Part I: Navigating the Net*. Here's a list of the basics covered in *Part I*:

1. Lost in Cyberspace (World Wide Web)
2. Write to the Prez (e-mail)
3. Chat, Chat, Chat (chat)
4. Lurking and Posting (Usenet newsgroups)

5. Future Forecast (mailing lists)
6. The Net Intelligentsia! (telnet)
7. Build Your Own Home (home pages)
8. Push Me! (push technology)
9. Plugged In (plug-ins)
10. Search, and Ye Shall Find (search sites)

Aside from covering the essentials, the first 10 chapters include a number of sites and resources to help you learn and explore on your own, such as My Excite Channel and My Yahoo! Read the first 10 chapters, experience the sites discussed in them, and you'll be a virtual netnaut, having learned the most important skills needed to navigate the Net. Once you're through with those chapters, you should have no problem browsing the rest of the book.

I've written this book in such a way that it should be useful to anyone with Internet access, whether you're connected through a national service provider, a local one, a university, or some other means. *50 Fun Ways to Internet* isn't geared for use with any specific type of computer or Internet connection. Whether you've got a PowerBook or a ThinkPad, whether you're connected through America Online or the local community college, you'll be able to use this book as a guide for traveling the Net. Some things may look slightly different, depending on the way you connect to the Net, but the same rules apply for using most tools and programs.

Well, no sense waiting—now's the time to start exploring the Net.

Part I

Navigating the Net

1

Lost in Cyberspace

Suffering from Net confusion? Wishing you could find a cyber-service to bring order to the vast amount of information on the Internet? Well, you're in luck. A number of sites will assist you in personalizing the Internet experience by highlighting the material you're most interested in viewing—the local weather forecast, say, or the scores from your favorite sports teams. Available on the area of the Internet known as the World Wide Web, these services, such as My Excite Channel and My Yahoo!, bring sanity to the sometimes anarchic world of the Net.

If you're not familiar with the Web, don't flee in fear. The World Wide Web may sound like a horror flick from the 50s ("Alien Spiders Land in Lansing!"), but it's actually a remarkable way of accessing information on the Net. Using the Web, you can move seamlessly from one document to another, weaving a web-like route among news headlines, mortgage calculators, dictionaries, art exhibits and online game shows.

To get a sense of the power of the Web, imagine you're researching a topic—the work of Pablo Picasso, say—and you're reading an essay about "Guernica," his commemoration of the destruction of a Spanish village. As you read the essay, you notice highlighted words and phrases—Cubism, Spanish Civil War, Franco. You know a few things about Cubism, but you'd like to learn more. You select the highlighted word, and a new document—a definition of Cubism—appears on your screen alongside an image of a Cubist painting. You read the definition, noticing other highlighted words, including the name Georges Braque, a contemporary of Picasso's. Select Braque, and your screen redraws with a short biography of the artist, who developed Cubism along with Picasso. The Web's power comes from the way it allows you to follow such connections, known as "links," in an intuitive manner dubbed "hypertext." Wandering around the Web, you move from one Web "page" to another, discovering new information.

To access My Excite Channel and My Yahoo!, start up the Web browser offered by your Internet service provider. The browser serves as your primary computer application for navigating the world of the Net. Most likely, you'll be using one of the two most popular browsers—either Microsoft Internet Explorer or Netscape Navigator.

Whatever browser you use, you'll need the address of a Web site to get anywhere on the Web. Each Web hotspot has its own home base, known as a "home page." To travel to a specific home page, you need a Web address, also called a URL (Uniform Resource Locator). Some sites, such as My Excite Channel (**http://my.excite.com**) and My Yahoo! (**http://my.yahoo.com**), have relatively simple URLs, while others have more complex ones. If you break into a sweat when you see a URL, try to overcome your fear. URLs can be extremely useful in finding information on the Net. Besides, you don't really need to know what all that gibberish means—you just need to know it will help get you someplace.

Once you've got your Web browser up and running, enter the URL for the Excite or Yahoo! sites. As you'll see, these pages offer the option of customizing the information for your needs. After you've personalized the site, you'll have something akin to your own daily newspaper. You're interested in stock quotes for Apple and AT&T? Excite and Yahoo! will oblige. Looking to have TV listings handy? No problem. Try out both of these pages, consider their features, and choose one as your home base for Web explorations.

2

Write to the Prez

Does the president read his e-mail? Does the vice president? Well, yes and no. As you might expect, they've got staffs to read the stuff. Staff members compile statistics on the utterances and blatherings of Netlanders, and they provide the president and vice president with the stats and a sampling of messages. But don't count on the prez logging onto his computer at midnight, reading your message, and saying, "Hey, I'm gonna write back to that guy." He's wired, but not that wired.

Electronic mail sent to the White House elicits a response from the 1984-esque "autoresponder." All autoresponses include information about the White House e-mail system and instructions for retrieving White House documents (see Chapter 35). The response from the president comes from an official whose lofty title is director of presidential e-mail. This guy knows his e-mail etiquette. Unlike the message from the veep's e-mail man, with its "Dear Friend" opening, the president's response begins without a salutation. Well, what else would you expect? A bureaucrat

-----

with "e-mail" in his title should know the way things work in Netland.

Like your own e-mail address, those of the nation's leaders—**president@whitehouse.gov** and **vicepresident @whitehouse.gov**—consist of three basic elements: a userame (**president** for the prez), the @ sign, and something called a "fully qualified domain name" (**white house.gov**). The fully qualified domain name—everything to the right of the @ sign—indicates a specific location on the Net (**aol.com** for those at America Online, for instance). The last piece of the address varies depending on the type of organization: **com** for commercial, **edu** for educational, **gov** for the U.S. government, **mil** for the U.S. military, **net** for major network centers and **org** for other organizations.

As you roam around cyberspace, pay attention to Internet addresses for what they tell you about your fellow netheads. Some, like **blaze@well.com**, may not tell you much, but others—**janedoe@harvard.edu**, say—provide clues about the person you're contacting.

3

Chat, Chat, Chat

It's three in the morning, you can't sleep, and your spouse (or your roommate or brother or pet) won't give up any Zs to hang out for a while and talk you into drowsiness. You get out of bed and put on your slippers. You're lonely. You wander around the house, stare into the fridge, inspect the dust balls gathering under the couch. Finally you turn on the TV. The lurid glow of an old *Gilligan's Island* spreads across the walls. You want company, but not Gilligan. So you turn off the tube and inspect the innards of the fridge one more time. Still the same: decaying broccoli, soy sauce, an apple. You walk into the den and turn on your computer. You want human companionship. You want to talk.

Is anybody out there?

Yes! Most definitely, yes!

Wherever you are, whatever time it is, you're not alone. If you want a companion for a midnight chat, you've got one—or two, or three, or a hundred. The Web's chat rooms allow people to connect from around the world and talk in "real time," even if the time is five in the morning in Ames, Iowa, and one in the afternoon in Helsinki, Finland.

In the early days of the Web, "live chat" meant learning to use the commands of Internet Relay Chat (see Chapter 45), but now a number of Web sites offer chat rooms, either through the use of a special "plug-in" (see Chapter 9 for details on plug-ins) or a small program, called an "applet," created with the Java programming language. Open24 (**http://chat.open24.net**) uses the Ichat plug-in to allow you to chat, as does Yahoo! Chat (**http://chat.yahoo.com**). There are other sites, such as EarthWeb Chat (**http://chat.earthweb.com**) and Talk.com (**http://www.talk.com**), that use Java-based interfaces. Most of these sites require you to have the latest Microsoft or Netscape Web browser.

One morning on Talk.com, WarandTraffic was asking Red~Silk, "Do you ever actually wear red silk?" Her response: "Have it on now, matter of fact."

Elsewhere, Lithia was saying she was "kind of sad," leading to a slew of "tell us all" questions.

Her problem? "my bf and i had a spat and now i can't get in touch with him. i'm worried." (It's kewl—uh, cool—to slide into lowercase, e.e. cummings mode in cyberspace chat.) Anyone who stayed tuned to her travails got to hear all about the fight. It got started, she said, when her "bf"— boyfriend, of course—failed to pick her up from work.

At Talk.com, as at most chat sites, you must register for a free account. Once registered, you enter your member name and password each time you return. The special features at Talk.com include the option of selecting several "nicknames" for yourself, the ability to "squelch" the talk of people you find annoying, and the chance to engage in "private chat" with newfound friends.

After you visit several of the Web's chat sites, try to find a place where you feel welcome. At the best chat sites, a community of "regulars" will often coalesce, bringing together like-minded people. But that doesn't always happen; sometimes, chat sites resemble a group of distracted people shouting inanities at each other. One site boasts of providing "a safe and comfortable place for meeting people and exchanging ideas." Meeting people, yes. Exchanging ideas? Well, I couldn't find any. Too often, the conversations in the Web's chat rooms don't offer much more than random blather. Here's a sample exchange:

```
WarandTraffic: why arent you working this week
red?
Red~Silk: i am sick again : (
WarandTraffic: sure you are. addicted to chat
maybe.
Red~Silk: haha.
```

And so on. Often, you'll see sentences scrolling down your screen, few of them making sense—or connecting with each other. It's as if 20 people were in a single room, having conversations with themselves.

Don't be surprised if someone asks you to enter a room for "private chat" during a visit to one of these sites. Should you? You can always leave. But, remember, lots of people are looking for romance, of a sort. If that's not your schtick, decline the offer. In fact, you can never be certain of the gender of the person you're meeting. At Yahoo! Chat, as at most other chat sites, you're encouraged to create a cyber-identity for yourself. Press the "Edit Identity" link, and you're a few keystrokes away from changing your age, marital status, and sex ("other" is an option). Strange, but true.

4

Lurking and Posting

If you want to get a sense of the diversity and strangeness of the Net, check out Usenet, a collection of thousands of electronic bulletin boards on topics ranging from angst to zines. In these bulletin boards, known as newsgroups, you'll find serious discussions (**alt.politics.datahighway**), not-so-serious discussions (**alt.peeves**), and a lot of discussions in the amorphous zone between the two (**alt.bitterness, rec.arts.comics.strips, talk.bizarre**). You can browse the newsgroups, not posting messages—a practice known as "lurking"—or you can jump right in, responding to whatever strikes your fancy.

Roam around Usenet, and you're likely to feel like you've come in contact with as odd and far-ranging an assortment of humanity as exists on the planet. One minute you'll be reading a message from someone theorizing about quarks in the **alt.sci.physics.new-theories** newsgroup, and the next minute you'll be reading about a plan to plot the death of a dinosaur in a group called **alt.barney. dinosaur.die.die.die**.

Methods vary for gaining access to newsgroups. In most cases, your Internet service provider will offer a "newsreader"—an application that allows you to select newsgroups, read messages, respond to messages and post new messages. Most newsreaders offer online instructions.

To begin, you must locate Usenet. On America Online, simply choose the keyword **internet** and click on the icon for newsgroups. If you're using Netscape Navigator or Communicator as your Web browser, look for the menu option for **Netscape News.** Whatever system you use, it shouldn't be difficult to locate Usenet—it's one of the most popular features of the Net.

Once you've found Usenet, look for an option that allows you to choose a newsgroup by its name. Most newsreaders offer such an option, and it's a very useful one, given that a list of the thousands of available newsgroups would take up screens and screens of information. To begin to explore Usenet, browse the messages, known as postings, in a newsgroup focused on books; type **rec.arts. books**, the group's name, as your selection. After entering the selection, you'll see a list of postings scroll down your screen:

```
Bronte Sisters?
W. Faulkner
THE LOST CONTINENT by Bill Bryson
Those wacky libertarians (gotta love 'em)
Tom Clancy
```

Each newsreader has its own look. Most include a title for each posting and the number of responses. By selecting a posting, you can read the initial message and the "thread" of responses to it; then, after you've read the item, you can respond.

As you'll discover by reading the postings to **rec.arts. books**, there's not a whole lot of "news" to read. While these bulletin boards have been anointed "newsgroups," the bulk of them focus on topics for discussion and argument; some serve as a forum for sharing information. That's not to say you can't find news, discuss news or even ask about a newsworthy event in a newsgroup. Even **rec.arts. books** can be a source for news. When the writer Charles Bukowski died, someone posted a message asking, "Is Charles Bukowski dead?" The trans-Atlantic response:

```
So said the French radio two days ago, if it
is considered as evidence.
```

In the realm of newsgroups, such a posting could develop into a full-fledged discussion of the author's work. Or, the thread could end with the first response. You can never tell what will set off a flurry of postings. Like most conversations, those in newsgroups can wander quite a bit. What starts as a discussion of the "My mother is a fish" chapter of Faulkner's *As I Lay Dying* may end up, many messages later, as a discussion of the depletion of fish in the waters of the Pacific Northwest.

While "news," in the traditional sense, does not dominate Usenet, a number of groups, especially those with a geographical focus (**soc.culture.china**, **soc.culture. mexican**, **soc.culture.palestine**), can be a source of information about events in those areas, particularly when something of import occurs. If there's a bombing in the West Bank, you're likely to find a discussion about it, and possibly some information not available on CNN.

The number of daily postings varies from group to group. Some groups, like **rec.arts.books**, get heavy traffic, with as many as 100 messages posted each day.

Others, like **rec.birds**, get just a few. But the volume doesn't always reflect the quality of conversation. Frequenting a group with hundreds of postings often means wading your way through a lot of drivel.

Moreover, each group has its own style and thematic bent. Take **rec.pyrotechnics**. Here you're likely to read messages about pipe bombs, firecrackers and grenade launchers. If you selected the posting on "fun camp tricks," you'd be treated to these responses:

```
Real easy and cheap attention-getter...take a
lighter and just toss it in a camp fire. Make
a nice boom.
```

```
When nobody is looking, put calcium carbide
in the campfire. Nothing happens until you
take a mouthful of water from your canteen
and spit it into the fire. Your companions
will stare in wonder at what you're drinking.
```

Yet another rather lengthy posting discussed an awe-inspiring stunt resulting in a flame shooting 60 feet into the air around a group of Boy Scouts. Probably no other group has as many postings with the word "kaboom" in them.

Rec.antiques, as you might expect, doesn't countenance discussions of people blowing up things. Instead, you're likely to find queries about Depression glass, antique toothpick holders, World War I militaria, or this one about early electric beaters:

```
I don't collect early kitchen appliances, but
it's been a long winter, with few estate
sales, and I just couldn't resist.
```

```
This thing is a "Dormeyer Electric Beater, US
Patent March 22, 1921 - Foreign Pats Pend,"
with a Hamilton Beach motor. It's
manufactured by The MacLeod Mfg. Co.,
Chicago.
```

```
The motor, which is a chunky cylinder about
3" in diameter and about 5" high...
```

You get the idea. These people take themselves seriously, as do the budding ornithologists in **rec.arts.birds**, as you can tell from the titles of their postings:

```
European Black Birds - Parent/baby relations
Pet Crows
Squirrel-proofing feeders
"Convincing" Sparrows to go elsewhere
Mystery birds?
I saw my first wild snow goose in Michigan!
```

Usenet's got something for everyone, that's for sure. You'll undoubtedly learn about human nature, if nothing else, from wandering around this place. It's an amateur anthropologist's paradise.

5

....

Future Forecast

....

You've taken a few trips to cyberspace, and you're
having a blast. You're thinking virtual reality, you're
thinking cyberpunk, you're thinking FAQs. In essence,
you're wired.

To become even more wired, consider subscribing to
the FutureCulture mailing list. Like a Usenet newsgroup,
a mailing list puts you in touch with people with similar
interests. In the case of FutureCulture, you get to hear
other people's musings about the future, especially as it
relates to technological developments and the virtual
community. The conversation ranges from talk about the
demise of communism to the problems of garbage incin-
eration to the ominous question, "Is the Net falling?"

Mailing lists tend to be more cohesive and less transi-
tory than newsgroups. To belong to a mailing list, you've
got to do something—subscribe—and that means com-
mitment. With Usenet, you can browse through postings
for a few minutes, maybe respond to one or two, and never
return. With a mailing list, you get mail from the group
every day, and you've got to deal with it, even if you just

6

The Net Intelligentsia

If you want to hang out with the coolest folks on the Net, check out the WELL, an online outpost based in the San Francisco Bay Area. Started in 1985 by the people who put out the *Whole Earth Catalog*, it has become one of the hottest spots on the Net, known for a genuine feeling of community and an eclectic assortment of "conferences." Members of the WELL, an acronym for Whole Earth 'Lectronic Link, think of this computer conferencing system as their online home. To them, the WELL is a "virtual community"—a place where people can meet, carry on interesting conversations and develop relationships. Spend an hour or two wandering around the WELL, reading the cerebral and literate discussions, and you'll see what they mean.

Before you travel to the WELL, you should know a few things about **telnet**, the program that will take you there—and to other destinations on the Internet. **Telnet** allows you to connect from your computer to other, more powerful computers on the Net, using a text-only interface. Once connected via **telnet**, you can use the terminal at your desk as if it were directly connected to the remote computer, whether it's a few miles away or around the globe. This gives you access to a lot of computing muscle. You'll want to **telnet** to another computer when that computer offers something unique, like an interactive game or a special chat system.

Most Internet service providers include a **telnet** application as one of the programs provided when you sign up. If you can't locate a **telnet** program among your other Internet applications, visit Shareware.com (**http://www.shareware.com**) and search for **telnet**; with Shareware.com (see Chapter 27), you'll be able to download a program to install on your system. The choices include SimpTerm for Windows and NCSA Telnet for the Macintosh.

To reach another computer with **telnet**, you must know the following information: the computer's name, a valid login name (if requested), and the password (again, if requested). How you initiate a **telnet** connection will depend on the specific program you're using, but it will generally entail entering a computer name and a port number: *computer_name port_number*. Not all **telnet** computers have a port number; if a port number is required, be sure to put a space between the computer name and the number.

For the WELL, **telnet** to **well.com** and log on as **guest**. You'll be dropped into an area designed to acquaint you with the community. From the WELL guest menu, you'll be able to learn about the WELL's history, read excerpts from conferences, and decide whether to register:

```
WELL GUEST MENU
1   What is the WELL?
2   What is a WELL Conference?
3   READ SAMPLES FROM THE WELL CONFERENCES
```

4   Access Information, Brochure, etc.

5   Leave a note for the WELL staff

6   Register for the WELL

As you can see, the guest account offers a user-friendly method for exploring the WELL.

Most people join the WELL for its more than 200 public and 100 private conferences. The names of these conferences include Unity, Virtual Reality, Whole Earth Review, Agriculture, Entrepreneurs, Buddhist, Dreams, Drugs, Ethics, Tibet, Berkeley, Couples, Disability, Generation X, Weird, House Music and Writers. Grateful Dead fans will encounter a bonanza of Dead talk, with public conferences on Deadlit, Feedback, Tapes, Tickets and Tours, and private ones titled Deadplan and Grapevine. Other private conferences on the WELL include Recovery, Women on the WELL, Readers' Circle, and WELL Writer's Workshop.

Each conference on the WELL is divided into separate discussions, called "topics." A topic begins with an opening statement, followed by responses. The conferences resemble Usenet newsgroups, with the "topics" similar to Usenet's titled postings, yet these conferences tend to have more focus and not as much random blather as most newsgroups. In many newsgroups, discussions don't gain much depth after a few postings, possibly because the people have such tenuous connections. At the WELL, the conversation often progresses and gains momentum within a topic, probably because the people have a feel for each other, a shared history of talking about a subject, and a sense of belonging.

The best way to get a sense of the WELL is to examine a conference or two. From the main menu of the guest account, select "READ SAMPLES." You'll be given a choice of discussions from the Grateful Dead conference, the Singles conference, the Veterans conference, and a few others.

Choose the Virtual Communities conference and check out "The WELL as a Community" topic. The topic begins with this question: "Is the WELL a community? How so? Or, why not?" From there you'll find a spirited discussion about the nature of virtual communities and the reasons why people think of the WELL as having—or not having, as the case may be—a strong sense of community.

As you'll learn from reading the conference excerpts, there's somewhat of a countercultural atmosphere to the WELL; it's definitely a California sort of place, with many members living in the Bay Area. WELLites even get together for parties—an unusual practice in the online world.

To become a member of the WELL, select "Register for the WELL" from the main menu of the guest account. Once you have your login name and password, you will use those—rather than **guest**—to gain access to the WELL. See you there! If you sign up, please say hello—my username is **blaze**.

7

....

Build Your Own Home

....

If you're a passive consumer of the information available on the Internet, then you're experiencing only half—
the lesser half, some might say—of the cyberspace experience. The Net is not simply about checking weather fore-
casts and reading news headlines, it's about sharing your
knowledge and your enthusiasms, and one of the most
powerful ways of doing that is by creating your own home
page.

Don't protest, claiming you don't know HTML—an acronym for hypertext mark-up language, the coding system
used to tell a Web browser how to display a Web page.
Plenty of tools exist to allow you to create Web pages without knowing HTML. Not only that, but several sites provide free space for Web pages, along with simple editors—
yes, free of HTML—for building basic Web sites.

Both GeoCities (**http://www.geocities.com**) and Tripod (**http://www.tripod.com**) provide free Web pages for
their members. Membership is free, and two megabytes of
space is allocated to each member—more than enough to
get you started. Both sites provide easy-to-learn tools for

building a home page. Essentially, you're able to create pages from your Web browser by choosing among various options presented to you. At Tripod, for instance, you're offered two different layouts for a home page, each with empty blocks where you're able to add images, text and lists of links to other sites. You can even choose the color scheme of the page. When you want to edit a page—or move or delete part of your nascent Web empire—you simply use Tripod's Homepage Housekeeper.

Of course, you may decide you want to learn more at some point—maybe you'll even begin experimenting with HTML (or a Web page editor, such as Microsoft FrontPage or Adobe Pagemill)—and you're free to do so at both Geo-Cities and Tripod.

Given that both sites offer pages for free, it's worth a visit to GeoCities and Tripod before deciding where to build your home on the Web. Aside from testing out their Web page editors, consider the online communities available at both sites. GeoCities is divided into "neighborhoods," with names like Area51 (science fiction and fantasy), Baja (four-wheeling, off-roading, adventure travel), Coliseum (sports and recreation), Hollywood (film and TV), Pentagon (military men and women), SoHo (art, poetry, prose) and WestHollywood (gay, lesbian, bisexual). Tripod, on the other hand, does not have specific neighborhoods or areas of interest, but the site does exude a friendly 20-something aura.

Once you've decided to create a home page, you've still got the hard work of producing something worth showing the world. Visit the pages at GeoCities and Tripod for ideas. People have used their free home pages for everything from personal zines and travelogues to wedding albums and advice columns. If you don't have your own brilliant idea, borrow someone else's, trying your own take on it.

8

Push Me!

Whoever coined the phrase "push technology" for one of the whiz-bang ways of finding information on the Internet clearly didn't run it by the marketing execs. Do you really want to have stories, photos and audio clips "pushed" onto your PC?

Apparently so, at least in the views of the techno-gurus at Microsoft Corp., Netscape Communications Corp. and several other Internet companies promoting "push" products. With push technology, content is delivered—or "pushed"—onto your PC from the Internet, generally when your computer is idle. With a push application installed on your machine, it's not necessary to "pull" material down from the Web when you want the latest stock quotes, news stories or weather reports.

Generally, when you're looking for information on the Internet, you have to find it on your own. You fire up your Web browser, then visit a Web site—ESPNET SportsZone (**http://espnet.sportszone.com**), say, for the latest on the Yanks. With push technology, you don't have to surf the Web for that information; the information is delivered to your machine when you're working on another project or away from your desk. Rather than saying to yourself, "Time to check the latest weather report"—and then visiting the Weather Channel (or another site)—a push program, once installed on your PC, will transfer that material (weather reports, sports scores, stock quotes) at regularly scheduled intervals, or whenever the information is updated. When you want to check the information, it will be available to you on your PC, saving you the time it would normally take to search for the information on the Net.

For people busy with other commitments, whether it's a meeting with clients or a ball game with the kids, the advantage is simple: You don't have to click through a series of Web sites. It's a bit like having the newspaper delivered, rather than having to go to the newsstand to buy a new copy each morning.

Whether or not you're a fan of push technology, you're likely to experience it, in one form or another, given the emphasis by the top two browser companies—Microsoft and Netscape—to provide push capabilities with their products. With the inclusion of push technology as part of the "package" you get when you buy or download your browser, push programs have taken a big step from being an Internet add-on to being an Internet essential. As with most applications with push capabilities, the Microsoft and Netscape products allow you to choose among "channels" of content, with material from those channels being delivered to your PC on a regular basis. For Microsoft's push product, visit **http://www.microsoft.com/ie**, a page devoted to Internet Explorer. For Netscape's, point your browser to **http://www.netscape.com** and look for links to Netcaster.

Of course, you need not use the push technology from Microsoft or Netscape. A number of companies, such as

BackWeb Technologies, Marimba Inc. and PointCast Inc., offer software to push content onto your PC.

The most established of the push products, the PointCast Network, delivers stories from sources such as CNN, the Boston Globe and Wired News, along with separate channels for health, sports and weather. PointCast functions like a screensaver, taking up much of your desktop when it's running. Stock quotes, headlines and ads scroll or flash on your screen, giving it more of a "broadcast" look than the typical Web page. To download PointCast, visit **http://www.pointcast.com** and follow the instructions. (It's available for both Macintosh and Windows computers.) Other companies offering push products include BackWeb (**http://www.backweb.com**) and Marimba (**http://www.marimba.com**).

The proponents of push technology—namely, the companies aiming to place their software and stories on your PC—say it brings simplicity to the anarchic ways of the Internet. Marimba boasts about the way users of its Castanet application, or "tuner," can now " 'tune in' to 'information channels' on a network in much the same way they tune in to their favorite television channels." The Castanet tuner periodically updates the channels, without the user even having to click on a remote: "If the received information is new software, the tuner can automatically update the appropriate program. If it's new content, such as a news story, users see it next time they view that channel... It's that simple."

Yes and no. Push technology has the potential to make the Net a more friendly place, especially for those weary of surfing to far-flung sites for information, but it's still in a relatively early stage of development. My advice: Try Castanet, PointCast and the other products, but one at a time. Even "push," with its aiming of simplifying the Net, can lead to information overload.

9

Plugged In

The Web site you're visiting says it's got lots of audio, video and animation, but when you click on the link for that whiz-bang multimedia presentation a message pops up telling you to visit another site to download a "plug-in," whatever that is.

Sound familiar? More and more often, Web sites require plug-ins for you to view the most interactive material they've got. With a plug-in installed on your PC, you're able to have an Internet experience that's closer to what you would view on a CD-ROM or a game installed on your hard drive: more action and audio, and less waiting for another Web page to appear on your screen.

The best Web sites let you know when a plug-in is required. If you don't have the plug-in, the site provides instructions on where to find it and how to download and install it. Still, it's possible you've lost track of what plug-ins you've got on your PC, if any, or what plug-ins were preinstalled with your Web browser. Whatever the case, you're likely to receive one of those "plug-in required" messages at some point in your Internet travels, considering that software companies have produced hundreds of plug-ins, with more on the way.

These plug-ins—small computer programs, in essence—work in tandem with your Web browser, extending its capabilities. Some plug-ins make it easier to view video over the Web. Others scan for viruses or allow you to "chat" with others in real-time. The most popular plug-ins include RealPlayer (**http://www.real.com**) and Shock-wave (**http://www.macromedia.com/shockwave**). Real-Player allows you to view and hear video and audio clips, while Shockwave is used primarily for animation, games and multimedia presentations. With the RealPlayer and Shockwave plug-ins installed on your machine, you'll have animation and video appearing directly in the window of your Web browser, rather than in a separate window or through the use of a "helper application."

For an up-to-date list of plug-ins, visit Browsers.com (**http://www.browsers.com**) and look for the plug-ins link on the home page. You can view the latest plug-ins and the most popular ones. And don't think you're just following the crowds by downloading the most popular plug-in. If a plug-in is popular, it's likely to mean there's a lot of interactive material created for it, as there is for the RealPlayer and Shockwave plug-ins.

Of course, once you've got your plug-ins installed, you're going to want to test them out in the real world (so to speak) of the Web. The following sites make the most of the RealPlayer and Shockwave plug-ins:

AudioNet

http://www.audionet.com

It's like having a radio (or even a TV) on your PC. News, music and talk, served up with on-demand (or live) audio and video. AudioNet's selection rivals what you'll find on the TV: concerts, interviews, sporting events, press conferences and full-length CDs. One minute you could be listening to an excerpt from General Douglas MacArthur's "Old Soldiers Never Die" speech, the next you could be jamming to Wu-Tang Clan or Tool.

CNET

http://www.cnet.com

This is a techno-site that's fun, friendly and for the rest of us. You don't need to know Java, C++ or any other computer language to understand CNET ("the computer network"). With its comparative reviews ("Seven PCs for Less Than a Grand") and "digital life" stories ("Law and the Web: What You Need to Know"), CNET helps you make sense of cyberspace. Its thoughtful use of the latest technology—audio interviews, scrolling news tickers and the like—makes CNET a model for others to emulate.

Mediadome

http://www.mediadome.com

"Webisodes" are created with a fearless use of the latest technology. An interactive feature about Duncan Sheik—hyped as a "musical legend in the making"—offers a "Journey through Duncan's Life," complete with a Shockwave profile, a video interview and clips from a Dallas concert. Given the site's high-profile partners—CNET and Intel—you can't help from feeling it's an experiment, albeit one that's worth your while.

Tunes.com

http://www.tunes.com

It's like one of those listening booths at all the big record stores, but controlled from your own PC. Search for an artist or record, and if it's current (and not too obscure), you'll probably find it, queued up and ready for listening. A clean and simple design, unlike so many Web stores.

Word

http://www.word.com

More than any other site, Word brings the best of the new-media gestalt to stories and art-pieces on current issues and culture. Much emphasis is placed on the site's look, as you'd expect—it's intuitive and atmospheric all at once—but with pieces produced and written by top talent. In "Slots of Fun with Bill," a series of moody black-and-white images rearrange themselves at your command, generating alternative narratives for your imagination to piece together. Go to the site with an open mind. Gaze at the future. What more could you want in a cyberspace zine for the next century?

10

Search, and Ye Shall Find

Here's your dilemma: You know there's got to be a Web site with the information you want—a copy of the Gettysburg Address, say, or a periodic table of the elements—but you're not sure where to find it. Usually, you would call your techie friend, but he's out of town, and you realize it's about time for you to learn how to find these things on your own. Is it possible? With so much on the Net, how do you find what you need? The answer is simple: You search.

Think of the Web's search sites as your gateway to the information strewn across the far-flung reaches of the Internet. Some search sites, such as Yahoo!, are organized as directories of Web sites, with categories such as Business, Computers and Sports. Other search sites—typically called "search engines" (AltaVista is among the most popular)—index the text appearing on Web pages. When you enter a keyword at AltaVista and press the Search button, Alta-Vista scans its index for all pages where that word appears. A search for **windows**, for instance, returned about 5,677,320 documents. A search for **beethoven** found 80,060 matches.

To search effectively, you need to learn a few techniques to help you narrow your queries. These techniques vary from site to site, but you can usually learn about them by looking for a link labeled "advanced" or "tips." At AltaVista, for instance, enclosing a query in quotation marks will narrow your search to a specific phrase.

A search for **"bruce springsteen"** will restrict the search to that phrase only (5,405 matches when I tried), while a search for **bruce springsteen** (without the quotation marks) will search for all pages with **bruce** and all pages with **springsteen**. Another way to narrow your search is to put a plus sign in front of the word you want to find. That will force AltaVista to return only those pages where that word appears. If I search for **+springsteen +badlands** (*Badlands* is the title of a Springsteen album), AltaVista will find only those pages with both words. You can combine the use of quotation marks and plus signs, as in **+"bruce springsteen" +badlands +"candy's room"**—a query that would search for only those pages with Bruce Springsteen, *Badlands*, and "Candy's Room" (the title of a song on the album *Badlands*). To exclude a word from your search, use a minus sign, much in the way you would use the plus sign: **+"bruce springsteen" +badlands -"candy's room"** (a search for pages mentioning Springsteen and *Badlands*, but not "Candy's Room").

Of course, even with these techniques, it's sometimes hard to find what you want. A search for **"tennis elbow"** gave me a list of 1,197 matches—the first page dealing with a study of "wrist kinematics," the second referring to the condition by its medical name (lateral epicondylitis), and the third sporting a huge ad for a suspicious-looking alterna-health remedy. With so much material on the Web, and the amount growing each day, the all-purpose search engines can be a morass of information, yielding thousands of links but little to differentiate what's valuable from what's not.

A number of search sites and directories have a solution. Rather than indexing everything on the Web, they target more narrow audiences (the counterculture crowd, as at Disinformation) and specific subjects (music sites, as at UnfURLed). In the early days of the Web, a site like Yahoo! was all you needed to search the Web.

Now, with every company on the globe peddling a product—and everybody and their brother publishing an e-zine—it helps to have access to search sites with a focus narrower than "anything on the Internet," which generally means more than you'd ever be able to read in a thousand lifetimes.

Yahoo!, aside from being a partner in UnfURLed, has sites for kids (Yahooligans!) and cities (Yahoo! New York, Yahoo! Los Angeles, and others). The "classic" Yahoo! remains useful, as do the other generic search sites, but the next time you set out to search, think about whether you're up for hours of clicking from site to site—or if you'd rather have a site present you with a more selective set of choices. (See Chapter 48 for more information on these subject-oriented search sites.)

For all your searching needs, here's a list of the best search sites on the Web:

AltaVista

http://www.altavista.digital.com

Speedy and powerful, especially if you learn a few tips for narrowing your search. A bare-bones interface, with few frills or extras. Quite often, that's what you want when you're scouring the Web.

Disinformation

http://www.disinfo.com

The motto: "The subculture search engine." In other words, the site's got a leftie bent, a skeptical attitude—categories include propaganda, revolutionaries, and counterintelligence—and a more selective archive of stories and sites than what you'll find elsewhere.

Excite

http://www.excite.com

The most intuitive and option-packed of the search sites, with lots of extras: live chat, free e-mail, and news and weather reports. An astounding amount of info, but you're never overwhelmed.

Health Explorer

http://www.healthexplorer.com

Reviews of more than 3,000 health-related Web sites, with thumbs-up signs highlighting the best sites. Search by keyword or browse among categories such as fitness, men's health, and nutrition.

HotBot

http://www.hotbot.com

A simple way to conduct sophisticated searches, especially if you want to limit your search to a person's name, a specific phrase, a time period, or even to a type of media (images, video, audio, and so forth).

Metasearch

http://www.metasearch.com

An easy-to-use gateway to AltaVista, Lycos, Yahoo! and other search sites. Enter your query, and Metasearch provides a series of option-packed forms for searching other sites. Handy when you want to see how different search sites handle a query.

Money$earch

http://www.moneysearch.com

Making sense of money on the Web. Brief reviews guide you to the top sites in categories such as banks, bonds, investment firms, online brokers, and taxes. Plus, stock quotes and business headlines.

Search.com

http://www.search.com

All sorts of search sites, on every topic imaginable (games, personals, recipes), gathered within an elegant, easy-to-use interface. Use it when you're searching for something specialized (a used car, say, or a new job).

UnfURLed

http://www.unfurled.com

The obvious choice when you're searching for music sites, reviews, and news. A partnership between MTV and Yahoo!, the site's got areas for artists, charts, genres, labels, and tours. Lots of "info booty," as UnfURLed puts it.

Yahoo!

http://www.yahoo.com

A subject-based directory of sites, with categories ranging from drinking games to employment law. Lots of adjuncts and extras, like Yahooligans! (for kids) and My Yahoo! (a personalized version).

Part II

....

Cruising the Net

....

11

The Art of the Flame

You know you're no longer a newbie once you've been flamed. Perhaps it's the quintessential Net initiation rite. You post a message—an erudite opinion on the convergence of the PC and the TV, say—and a fellow Net traveler responds with words a family publication wouldn't print. And you wonder: *What did I do wrong? Why do I deserve this?* You don't, but not everyone's in favor of netiquette. Some people like to flame, to spew verbal vitriol at their comrades in Netland. It's discouraged in many forums, but not all. In fact, there's a site on the Net—**alt.flame**, a Usenet newsgroup—where people go to flame and be flamed.

Alt.flame has its own skewed logic. You come to **alt.flame** to be flogged, berated, spit upon, harassed; you know what you're getting and why you're there. Believe it or not, this is popular, a hit on the Net. It's not uncommon for 150 new messages to be posted in the course of a day. What does it all mean? Why this fervor for abuse and self-abuse? I don't know, but I'm sure it's a ripe subject for a doctoral dissertation: *Alt.flame and the Joan of Arc Archetype.* Or something like that.

One visitor to **alt.flame** asked a reasonable question, a dangerous practice in this realm of epithets: "Are you all whacked, or what?"

```
You know, I was wondering: What kind of
antisocial cretin came up with the idea of a
newsgroup that does nothing constructive,
nothing positive, and nothing *WORTH READING*?!
Are you all malcontents with nothing better to
do than rank on other people with racial slurs
and unintelligent insults, or is this just a way
of venting your frustrations?
```

Notice the way this **alt.flame** newbie and critic, even as he questions the existence of **alt.flame**, does some flaming himself, calling alt.flamers "antisocial cretins" and "malcontents." He may do well in **alt.flame**. He got this response:

```
Here, in alt.flame, we sharpen our wits, strive
to be the first with the good ol' snappy
comeback. It's fun. Think of it as one big game
of chess, who can outmaneuver whom, who gets on
top and stays there. There _is_ a certain sick
thrill attached to it, but take nothing
personally. Relax and join us in a good ol'
chuckle at someone else's expense, knowing that
person has willingly entered the arena, and is
totally cognizant of the risks within, and if
defeated, will wait and try to do the same to
you down the road.
```

Alt.flamers revel in humiliating each other; it's central to the zeitgeist of the place. They take a great deal of pride in what they do. It's not uncommon for the denizens of **alt.flame** to refer to "professional flamers" or an "artful flame," as if flaming is the highest, most noble form of expression. This is serious business, with everyone competing for the most creative epithets: "mewling newbie nobody," "banal bozo," or the rather dull "grade-school slob." Usually it takes a few more words to flame with full force, as this alt.flamer displays:

> You're another lower echelon loser that will
> never break out of ranks of the mundane. You
> will always just be the noise lost in the
> background, the killfile fodder of thousands,
> the boring, yammering little shit desperately
> pulling on the trouser leg of the professional
> flamer.

If you're going to visit **alt.flame**, you should have something to say, and you should say it with venom. Other forums on the Net advocate an atmosphere of rational discourse: criticize the idea, but not the person. No such rule exists at **alt.flame**. If you have a fragile ego, beware—this isn't the place for you. Here's a sampling:

> Once again you've proven beyond a shadow of a
> doubt that you're nothing but an incoherent,
> gibbering, slack-jawed gibbon with absolutely
> nothing noteworthy to say. Shouldn't you be
> getting back to the monkey cage at the Denver
> zoo? I'm sure your parents are worried sick...

> Your posts probably closely reflect your
> miserable, sex-starved existence.

> Your direct low-brow monosyllabic retorts to my
> artful flames shows the world you are merely a
> single-celled lifeform.

Like the postings themselves, the titles to them should be flamish, if at all possible:

> My days of being an Anonymous Chickenshit
> Poster...

> I love to be flamed

> A Supreme COMMUNIST Plot TO DESTROY THE
> WEST!!!!!

```
HAHAHAHAHAHA FRANK ZAPPA IS DEAD!!!!!!!!
Bowling is the Pope's vice
Mock Turtles die in Vain
```

These people aim to offend, but they're creative, too—you've got to give them that. Visit **alt.flame**, but be forewarned: Everything you say will be held against you.

12

Netiquette

When you walk into a shop in Paris to buy your baguette, you say *bonjour* to the proprietor. When you meet an acquaintance in Safeway, you say "hello" and ask about friends and family. And when you've got something to say on the Net, you post your message selectively; you don't want to commit a major *faux pas* by sending it to every Usenet newsgroup from **alt.alien.visitors** to **talk. politics.tibet**.

Like any culture, the Net has its customs, and it's best to abide by them. You don't send e-mail in ALL CAPS. You don't flame without good reason. You don't send unsolicited messages to hundreds of thousands of cybercitizens. In short, you try to adhere to the rules of netiquette.

If you think of the Net as a lawless land, where anything goes, you're only partly right. Yes, you're certain to encounter bad behavior on the Internet, as in other spheres of life, but that doesn't mean you shouldn't learn the accepted rules of conduct. In fact, the Web offers a number of guides to proper Internet etiquette (a.k.a. netiquette).

The most established source for such information, (**http://www.fau.edu/rinaldi/netiquette.html**), was written by Arlene H. Rinaldi of Florida Atlantic University with the aim of ensuring that users act responsibly in their online communications. It includes sections on etiquette for e-mail, mailing lists, newsgroups and the Web, along with "The Ten Commandments for Computer Ethics" from the Computer Ethics Institute ("Thou shalt not use a computer to steal," "Thou shalt not appropriate other people's intellectual output," etc.).

Much of the advice might be categorized as common sense ("Keep your questions and comments relevant to the focus of the discussion group"), but people often disregard the rules, with some forums dominated by endless off-topic rants. If more people read Rinaldi's guide, the level of discourse on the Net might be a bit higher.

For an amusing take on netiquette, try Dear Emily Postnews (**http://www.clari.net/brad/emily.html**). Written in the style of an advice column, Emily—actually Brad Templeton, the publisher of ClariNet Communications Corp.—composes sardonic answers to stupid questions, like this one: "Somebody just posted that Roman Polanski directed *Star Wars*. What should I do?"

The response: "Post the correct answer at once! We can't have people go on believing that! Very good of you to spot this. You'll probably be the only one to make the connection, so post as soon as you can."

The exchanges in Dear Emily Postnews, while amusing, can also teach you something about what's acceptable—and what's not—on the Net:

```
Dear Emily Postnews: I saw a long article that I
wish to rebut carefully, what should I do?

A: Include the entire text with your article,
particularly the signature, and include your
```

comments closely packed between the lines. Be
sure to post, and not mail, even though your
article looks like a reply to the original.
Everybody *loves* to read those long point-by-
point debates, especially when they evolve into
name-calling and lots of "Is too!"—"Is not!"—"Is
too, twizot!" exchanges.

The lesson: A point-by-point rebuttal of an article or
post, especially with the previous message included in your
own, can inspire a lot of ire in your fellow surfers.

13

The Virtual World

You find yourself standing at the edge of a kitchen patio surrounded by shimmering roses. Your hand shades the glare of the midday sun and you gaze at a swimming pool in the distance. It's hot. You wouldn't mind taking a dip. You hop onto the diving board and jump in the pool, thrashing about in the murky water. You bump into a green plastic snake, an air mattress, and a hypercube tub toy, whatever that is. Then, you notice the shark cage...

You've just taken a trip to a place called LambdaMOO, one of the hundreds of "virtual worlds" being settled on the electronic frontier. Known as MUDs, MUSHes, MOOs, and an ever-changing host of M-words, these alternative realities allow you to explore otherworldly environments and interact with the inhabitants. Type **open door** from LambdaMOO's coat closet, and a description of a living room—"bright, open, and airy"—scrolls down your screen. Type **jump** while you're on the pool deck, and you'll see "Splash!" and a list of objects, like that hypercube tub toy, floating on surface. Type **say I'm wet—hand me a towel**, and "I'm wet—hand me a towel," with your character's name attached to it, will appear on the computers of anyone else out for a swim. At LambdaMOO, you can build a home for yourself, carry on conversations with fellow MOOers, and generally let your imagination run wild in a free-for-all of text-based virtual reality.

LambdaMOO and its brethren in cyberspace have names like ThunderDome, Dud, Longhorn, Mozart and Synergy, each with its own aura of weirdness. Many of these M-things have the characteristics of role-playing games, with participants accumulating points as they cast hexes and throttle each other with weapons. Others have moved beyond the game paradigm and into a realm where the inhabitants don't compete so much as hang out, experiencing what it's like to invent and occupy a collaboratively imagined world. MUDs—the acronym stands for Multi-User Dungeon (or, some say, Multi-User Dimension)—tend to emphasize game-like qualities, often reflecting their roots in the world of Dungeons & Dragons. MOOs (MUD Object Oriented), on the other hand, place more weight on social interaction, whether it's playing Twister™ at LambdaMOO or taking a college-level class at a MOO called Diversity University (see Chapter 23). You're more likely to have a conversation on a MOO, and less likely to have someone pierce your armor with a lance—a more MUD-like occurrence.

To get a feel for the virtual world, take a trip to Xerox Corporation's Palo Alto Research Center, where Lambda MOO, one of the most unique multi-user environments, was developed by Pavel Curtis. As described by its creators, "LambdaMOO is more of a pastime than a game in the usual sense. There is no 'score' kept, there are no specific goals to attain in general, and there's no competition involved. LambdaMOO participants explore the virtual world, talk to the other participants, try out the weird gadgets that others have built, and create new places and things for others to encounter and enjoy."

To enter the world of LambdaMOO, **telnet** to **lambda. moo.mud.org 8888**. A welcome message will scroll down your screen. "LambdaMOO is a new kind of society," it says, "where thousands of people voluntarily come together from all over the world. What these people say or do may not always be to your liking; as when visiting any international city, it is wise to be careful who you associate with and what you say." Type **connect Guest**, and you'll be dropped into a coat closet:

```
connect Guest
*** Connected ***
The Coat Closet
The closet is a dark, cramped space. It appears
to be very crowded in here; you keep bumping
into what feels like coats, boots, and other
people (apparently sleeping). One useful thing
that you've discovered in your bumbling about is
a metal doorknob set at waist level into what
might be a door.
```

As you're crouching in the coat closet, wondering what to do next, you may see others arriving and heading into MOOland:

```
Cyan_Guest has connected.
Cyan_Guest opens the closet door and leaves,
closing it behind itself.
Strange things may happen around you:
Brown_Guest comes home.
You hear a quiet popping sound; Brown_Guest has
disconnected.
zzyzx* flattens out into a largish 29 cent
postage stamp and floats away.
```

```
Ochre_Guest has connected.
A largish 29 cent postage stamp floats into the
room and fattens up into zzyzx*.
```

Don't worry about any of this—it's business as usual on the MOO. Occasionally, words may appear on your screen as you're typing a command of your own. If that happens, just keep typing; your commands won't be affected by the descriptions of people coming and going and turning into postage stamps. (If you get stuck and want to leave, you can disconnect at any time by typing **@quit**.)

Before exploring LambdaMOO any further, you should know what to do if you're lost or confused. Typing **help** will provide general help information. If you want help on a specific topic, type **help** *topic*. (For a list of available topics, type **help index**.) Don't be shy about asking for help. With odd beings and objects all around you, you're likely to become disoriented as you begin to familiarize yourself with the place.

Typing **help manners** will provide you with information on MOO etiquette. "LambdaMOO, like other MUDs, is a social community," you're told. "It is populated by real people interacting through the computer network. Like members of other communities, the inhabitants of Lambda MOO have certain expectations about the behavior of members and visitors." You're asked to follow "two basic principles of friendly MOOing: let the MOO function and don't abuse other players."

Wizards rule the world of MOOs. Because of this, you don't want to do anything to inspire the ire of the wizards. Any action that "threatens the functional integrity of the MOO, or might cause legal trouble for the MOO's supporters, will get the player responsible thrown off by the wizards." Like the real world—a place netnauts call irl (in real life)— MOOs have social problems. At LambdaMOO, these include

---

71

"spamming" (filling someone's screen with unwanted text), "teleporting" (moving a character or its objects without consent), and "spoofing" (causing messages to appear without attribution to your character). "The MOO is a fun place to socialize, program and play as long as people are polite to each other," according to the manners help file. "Rudeness and harassment make LambdaMOO less pleasant for everyone."

Once you know how to conduct yourself on the MOO and ask for help, try moving around the place. To do this, you type a direction or open a door. Most descriptions of rooms, like the coat closet, include clues about how to leave. The coat closet description calls attention to a metal doorknob. Other rooms indicate exits with compass points such as **east**, **northeast**, **south**, and so on, along with **up**, **down** and **out**. Using these commands is simple and intuitive. If you want to move east, type **east**. If you want to go down, type **down**. To leave the closet, type **open door**:

open door

You open the closet door and leave the darkness for the living room, closing the door behind you so as not to wake the sleeping people inside.

The Living Room

It is very bright, open, and airy here, with large plate-glass windows looking southward over the pool to the gardens beyond. On the north wall, there is a rough stonework fireplace. The east and west walls are almost completely covered with large, well-stocked bookcases. An exit in the northwest corner leads to the kitchen and, in a more northerly direction, to the entrance hall...

Now you're in the living room, with people talking, giggling and having a pillow fight:

```
Marglenna takes out a previously unseen fluffy
white pillow.
Syntax says, "Cause I'm Syntax and I'm ouutaaaa
heeeeere."
Rhiannon smiles at Chewy.
Babs laughs really hard in real life!
Marglenna then proceeds to beat Purple_Guest
silly with it.
Babs says, "so anyway..."
Rhiannon notices K'ra looking at her...she
smiles shyly and returns to her conversation.
Babs giggles at Laila.
```

If you want to join this conversation, express your reaction to it, or move onto another room, you're going to need to know how to use three essential MOO verbs—**look**, **say** and **emote**. These verbs, and others used by more experienced MOOers, help you move around the MOO and control your actions.

Look is one of the most frequently used MOO commands. It's especially helpful to MOO newbies, who often get lost and need an easy way to reorient themselves. To see where you are, type **look** and you'll get a description of your location. **Look** can also be used to learn about an object in a room. If you want to see an object—one that's mentioned in a room's description—type **look** *object*. If you're in the dining room, you may notice an object called Twister™. Type **look Twister**, and you'll see a description of "the classic party game Twister with seven colors and a spinner."

To speak, use the form **say** *What you want to say*. If you type **say I'm new here. What's up?**, you'll see **You say, "I'm new here. What's up?"** on your screen. If your name were Verve—my name on the MOO—others in that room would see **Verve says, "I'm new here. What's** up?" You can also speak by typing a quotation mark, followed by what you want to say:

```
"I'm lost. Help!
You say, "I'm lost. Help!"
```

You can indicate nonverbal communication (smiles, frowns, etc.) with the emote command. If I type **emote turns his head and stares at the sky**, my fellow MOOers—those in the same location as me—will see **Verve turns his head and stares at the sky**. You can replace **emote** with a colon. If I type, **:ducks to avoid the pillow**, others will see **Verve ducks to avoid the pillow**.

As a guest on the MOO, you'll be given a name, probably something like **Cyan_Guest** or **Brown_Guest**. If you decide, after wandering around for a while, that you like LambdaMOO, you should acquire a character of your own. With your own character, you'll be able to participate more fully in the MOO by building objects and rooms. To acquire a character, decide on a name—strange names rule the MOOworld—and type:

@request *character_name* **for** *your_email_address*

LambdaMOO is a busy place, with rules about the number of new characters it will issue, and you may be put on a waiting list. Once your request is processed, general information on the MOO and a password will be sent via e-mail.

After you get your character, **telnet** to LambdaMOO and log on with the command **connect** *character password*. As a bonafide character at LambdaMOO, you get to describe yourself with the commands **@describe** and **@gender**. To use **@describe**, type **@describe me as** *description*. If I type **@describe me as** "Tall, slim, cool," anyone who types **look Verve** will see the following:

```
Verve
Tall, slim, cool
It is awake and looks alert.
```

Notice that I'm called "it." To change that, I can set my gender with the command **@gender** *gender_of_choice*. I decided to be a man on the MOO, using the command **@gender male**. Now the MOO will use male pronouns when referring to me.

LambdaMOO offers an excellent tutorial for learning about the MOO. It's well-worth the time, especially since many other M-things use the software of LambdaMOO, meaning the skills you learn here will be applicable elsewhere. To start the tutorial, type **@tutorial**.

14

Search for a Long-Lost Friend

An Illinois man sat at his computer one night and searched Switchboard, a phone directory on the World Wide Web, for a woman living in Oklahoma. Within seconds, he had the number. Nervous about calling her—he believed she was his biological mother—he waited five minutes, then made the call.

On his first try, he got her machine. He hung up. After all, this wasn't something you leave on a person's answering machine.

A half-hour later, he tried again. This time, she answered.

"Does Jan. 21, 1964, mean anything to you?" he asked.

At first, she said it did not. Then, after a pause, "Yes."

"Did you place a baby boy for adoption?"

"Yes."

"Well," the man said, "you're talking to him."

"I'm so glad you found me," she told him.

An exceptional story, without a doubt, but one that is increasingly common. Most people don't search the

Internet for their mothers, but they do use Switchboard and other services to find people they want to contact. With the vast amount of personal information available on the Internet, including national "white pages" listings with phone numbers and street addresses, it doesn't take much effort to track down college roommates, old boyfriends and girlfriends, or old Army buddies.

Much of the information now on the Net has been available for years, but it was often scattered among different sources, like libraries and private databases. Now it's all in one place. Not only that, it's easily accessible and simple to use.

Still, tracking down someone can take some creative detective work. The man who found his adoptive mother, like most cyber-sleuths, employed a number of techniques—some virtual, some not. With the information he had from his adoptive parents, he found her in a high school yearbook. Next, he called the senior class president to see if he knew her whereabouts. But it was entering her name at Switchboard (**http://www.switchboard.com**), a white pages directory, that cinched it for him.

The white pages have been around for quite a while, but not many people would be willing to search through scores of phone books to find a friend. Now, Web sites such as Switchboard put the listings all in one place. These directory services, along with others offering business listings and more extensive investigative services, make the Internet the people-finding tool of choice for many. Often, it's being used to connect people who wouldn't have gotten in touch otherwise.

When the Internet was first gaining in popularity, a cartoon in *The New Yorker* showed a dog in front of a computer screen. It said, "On the Internet, nobody knows you're a dog." But that's not as true as it once was. For the most part, the days of the Internet as a freewheeling world of anonymity have come and gone. Now, people on the Net not only know that you're a dog, they know what breed of dog you are. And, most likely, they know your street address, phone number, and e-mail address. At some sites, it's possible to locate a person's name and, with the press of a button, get directions to the person's house. Another click, and you've got a map of the town.

If you're looking to find a person on the Internet, your best bet would be to start with a site like Switchboard or Four11 (**http://www.Four11.com**), two of the Web's most popular directories. Other choices include: Bigfoot (**http://www.bigfoot.com**); The Internet Address Finder (**http://www.iaf.net**); WhoWhere (**http://www.whowhere.com**); and Worldpages (**http://www.worldpages.com**). Enter a name and other information, such as a city or organization, and soon, if you're lucky, you'll have a list of results.

Most of these sites gather information from white pages listings and other publicly available sources. Some of them offer quick connections between e-mail addresses, phone numbers, and street addresses, but others, citing privacy concerns, only provide links between e-mail addresses and other information with permission from the individual. Most people, after all, don't make their phone numbers available with the idea of an e-mail address being attached to it.

Other Web directory sites allow you to find the phone numbers and addresses of businesses and other organizations. The top choices among these yellow pages sites include BigBook (**http://www.bigbook.com**) and BigYellow (**http://www.bigyellow.com**). The services vary from site to site, but generally they allow you to search for a business by entering a combination of the name, category of business and location. Many sites also offer maps and travel directions.

If you're looking for more extensive information about a person, and not just an e-mail address or phone number, you might want to consider visiting AltaVista (**http://www.altavista.digital.com**), Lycos (**http://www.lycos.com**), or one of the Web's other search engines (see Chapter 10). These sites archive material across the Web, including everything from personal home pages to newspaper stories to course schedules. When searching these sites, it's best to restrict your search by using distinctive information, such as an organization name, a place, or another word likely to appear in a document with the name of the person you're trying to locate; otherwise, you may end up with too many "matches" for them to be of any use.

The ability to search the Internet in so many different ways raises a number of concerns about privacy, especially when many people, such as those participating in discussion forums, may not realize their words will be archived and made available for others to search. Consider the Usenet newsgroups, where people talk about everything from object-oriented programming to sexual fantasies. Many of the participants in these discussions don't realize their words will be archived. Not only that, anyone can visit a site like DejaNews (**http://www.dejanews.com**), type in a person's name—or even an e-mail address—and find everything the person said in any number of newsgroups.

Given the concerns about privacy, some directory sites have created ways to help the denizens of the Internet retain some degree of privacy. A number of sites offer individuals control over their listings. At Switchboard, you can decide whether to have your e-mail address included with your listing. You can also choose to have your listing removed altogether. Another option, called Knock-Knock,

allows you to choose Switchboard to act as a conduit for
e-mail messages. If you're "found" by someone at Switchboard, the person will not see your e-mail address; instead,
a message from that person will be routed to you via
Switchboard. Only when you reply to the message will
your e-mail address be revealed to the person contacting
you.

Industry leaders say they recognize the importance of
offering people choices in how their personal information
appears on the Internet. The most popular directories,
such as Four11 and Switchboard, allow people to add information—high school graduating class, fax number, and
so forth—to their databases. Or, if they choose, to limit
what others can learn.

Privacy experts say it's wise to remain vigilant about
what personal information you provide about yourself on
the Net, whether to private companies or in public discussion forums. Too many people believe they can hide behind
the facade of a generic-sounding e-mail address. That may
have been true in the early days of the Internet, but now
it's not nearly as easy to remain anonymous.

15

Networking Party

The Internet's discussion areas get a bad rap. Most people think of them as spots for inane chat and unwanted solicitations, where the conversation rarely rises above the level of *Beavis and Butthead*. The stereotype may be true for some forums, but not all of them. And in one area—career-related networking—the Net excels in its ability to bring together professionals with different backgrounds and experiences, all of them sharing their knowledge.

Many of the Internet's best spots for networking are e-mail lists and newsgroups established for the discussion of a specific topic, such as the programming language Perl, freelance writing or Web development. These forums are useful for education and information—often, the top experts in the field participate—but they're also an excellent way to hear about job opportunities and make contacts with your peers.

One particularly active e-mail discussion group, the World Wide Web Artists Consortium mailing list (**http://wwwac.org**), receives scores of messages each day on everything related to producing sites for the Web. People talk about the top tools for creating Web pages. They argue about push technology and the different models for advertising on the Web. And they talk quite a bit about who's hiring, who's not, and the general direction of an industry still in its youth. The list has the feel of a networking party, where people are exchanging gossip, arguing about the latest news, and making contacts to pick up assignments or land a new job.

Some discussion areas have a more educational focus, but that doesn't mean they're not useful for networking. At the **comp.lang.java.programmer** newsgroup, the conversation leans more toward helping fellow programmers, with posts labeled "Compiler Problems" and "Platform-independent Fonts." Still, assisting your peers can certainly help when you're looking for work or exploring job possibilities.

Aside from mailing lists and newsgroups, a lot of networking occurs within various online communities, such as the WELL (see Chapter 6) and the career-specific forums on America Online and CompuServe. At the WELL, a pioneering online community that's still got a strong following, participants can choose between various conferences, such as those for advertising and freelance journalism. In the Byline conference, journalists ask each other advice on everything from buying a fax machine to locating expert sources. Of course, there's also a topic for job sightings and assignments.

Finding a forum for your career of choice can be a challenge in itself. Ask colleagues if they know of any, or visit Web sites of organizations associated with your field. If those tactics fail, search CyberFiber (**http://www.cyber fiber.com/news/**) or Tile.Net (**http://www.tile.net/**) for relevant forums.

16

Finding a FAQ!

Among all of the information-packed resources available on the Net, from searchable dictionaries to the works of William Shakespeare, one of the simplest remains the most useful. FAQ documents—compilations of frequently asked questions (and answers)—offer information and advice, most of it from nonexperts, on everything from backgammon to brewing your own beer.

Don't mistake a FAQ for the sort of information you'll find in an encyclopedia or a carefully researched reference guide. Some FAQs are written by professionals, but most are not. The FAQ for coffee and caffeine offers a caveat: "This information was excerpted from several sources. No claims are made to its accuracy. The FAQ maintainer is not a medical doctor and cannot vouch for the accuracy of this information."

Fair enough. Like most FAQ documents, the one on coffee and caffeine doesn't pretend to provide definitive answers. Rather, it's a way of sharing the experiences of people who consume lots of caffeine. You'll find suggestions for "caffeine fading"—cutting down gradually—and charts with the amounts of caffeine in popular beverages.

Many FAQs have their origins in the freewheeling discussions of Usenet newsgroups. The people who frequent newsgroups often see the same questions posted again and again. The answers to these questions, gathered together, form a substantial, if largely homegrown, base of knowledge. Instead of repeating the same answers, a newsgroup regular volunteers to assemble the questions and answers into a FAQ document, which is then posted to the newsgroup every month or so.

One such FAQ, for inline skating, had its origins in the **rec.sport.skating.inline** newsgroup. Available at **http://www.skatefaq.com**, the inline skating FAQ answers questions about stopping, skating backwards, racing, and just about everything else on the sport. In a section on skating down stairs, the FAQ provides suggestions and opinions from various skaters, most of them highly enthused about sharing their own techniques and experiences. One person advised caution: "It should be understood that if you push beyond the level of your abilities, and you happen to land on your head, even with a helmet, you could kill yourself."

Aside from coffee and inline skating, the Net has FAQs on hundreds of other topics—breastfeeding, diabetes, oral hygiene, *Saturday Night Live* and Scrabble, just to name a few. You'll find FAQs on serious subjects (adoption, depression) and not-so-serious subjects (the writer Dave Barry).

Two Internet sites make it easy to find FAQ documents. Usenet FAQs (**http://www.cis.ohio-state.edu/hypertext/faq/usenet/FAQ-List.html**) lists them alphabetically, while the FAQ Finder (**http://ps.superb.net/FAQ/**) allows you to search for a specific subject or scan lists of categories, such as art, games, religion, sports, and TV shows.

17

Love, Cyberstyle

The Net is not a sexless place. Just the opposite, as a matter of fact. Sex is everywhere on the Net. It's in newsgroups, it's in mailing lists, it's coursing through telephone wires across the world even as you read this. You can't go far on the Internet without bumping into a sex-related something, even if you don't expect it. If you want sex—real or simulated, if such a distinction still applies—you've got your choice of destinations on the Net.

Alt.personals is a freewheeling newsgroup devoted to connecting people across Netland. The postings to **alt. personals** range from the conventional ("DWF in Silicon Valley Seeking Mr. Right!") to the downright strange. Many of them describe desires in the most explicit terms. Some include anatomically detailed descriptions. You'd be surprised, the things people say—and admit to—on the Net. Take this posting:

```
I seek a sensual and sexy older woman that
enjoys teasing and seducing a younger man and
revels in the act of shedding her pillar of the
community reputation to satisfy her lustful
desires.
```

And how about this one:

```
OK, I'm not a computer geek, so if you are keep
going. I'm a 19 yr. old white male looking for
hot casual sex with an attractive lady. I am a
Los Angeles writer/actor attending school right
now. I'm not some desperate loser, I just love
good sex. I promise a good time and good looks.
You won't be disappointed. The ugly need not
apply.
```

Modesty, it seems, is not an attribute of the frequent-ers of **alt.personals**:

```
YOU WANT ME
Girls! Stop here and I can save you some
precious time!
Any sluts for stud service?
```

And people don't try to cover up their desperation:

```
need sex...NOW
Horny
```

Yet it's not just a place for undersexed college students seeking a few thrills. You get all types, like the kid from Berkeley who posted a message with the label "14-year-old SWM seeks nerdy SWF about same age." A self-described "mediocre violinist" and "computer geek," this 14-year-old was looking for a "partner," for "females around my age with the same interests." He listed his levels of proficiency in various computer languages: C, C++, various LISP dia-lects, MIPS R2000 assembly.

Posters should avoid going overboard with acronyms, like these clowns:

```
28 SWM, 25, ISO SWF DC area
29 SWM(28) ISO SWF(23-30) in NM
```

30 SWM ISO S/M/WF or WC IN DC METRO AREA

31 SWM seeks SWF, TX,AR, MS,LA,OK,TN

Of course, **alt.personals** isn't just a place for finding a Net partner. Posters to **alt.personals** don't hold back; they ask whatever's on their minds. One young man, apparently suffering from earring anxiety, brought this question to **alt.personals**: "Is an earring worn in a male's right ear a reliable sign of his being gay?" Within a few days, he got answers from across the world, with Internet wanderers offering their knowledge of customs in the States and elsewhere. Ask a question like that one, and you're likely to get a few erudite answers, like these two, with socio-historical perspectives on the topic:

> It used to be that gay guys wore an earring on
> the left, but that got adopted by a lot of guys,
> and now you're as likely to see one on a high
> school football player at the mall with his
> girlfriend as you are on anyone. Then gays moved
> to the right ear, but there are so many guys of
> alternative lifestyle, of every sexuality, that
> have them in either or both ears, or multiple
> earrings, that it's no longer safe to assume
> anything about a dude's sexuality from his
> earrings. That is, unless the earrings are
> little pink triangles.

There was a time when wearing an earring PERIOD
was considered a reliable sign. Now, dozens of men
wear them. Same thing with the right ear. It was a
reliable sign but more and more men are wearing
them.

> I rather like the idea, it gender-f**ks
> everyone. Besides, what difference should
> someone's orientation make?

"Personals," in the traditional sense, may dominate **alt.personals**, but feel free to ask any question of a personal nature, like the one about giantess fantasies:

> Most cultures have folklore with giants, but few
> have giantesses. One can think of numerous
> reasons for this (most of them sexist). As
> societies become more liberal women seem to be
> identifying more with images of strength—women's
> body building seems to have entered the
> mainstream, as an example.
>
> The question is—would women who feel comfortable
> with power identify with giantesses?

Where else could you discuss such a topic?

No one knows how many people connect through **alt.personals**, and whether those connections result in anything other than thousands of infonauts typing frantically in front of the dull glow of their 60-megahertz machines, but it's certainly an active forum. I tend to believe a Net romance is more likely to develop in a more contemplative setting, like **rec.arts.books**, than in the desperate land of **alt.personals**. With that caveat, here's a list of other places to look for sex, or partners, on the Net:

alt.sex.bestiality	The ASPCA is not amused.
alt.sex.bondage	Keep your leather handy.
alt.sex.fetish.feet	No comment.
alt.sex.motss	Members of the same sex.
alt.sex.stories	Will this put Penthouse Forum out of business?
alt.sex.wanted	Like alt.personals, but more explicit.
soc.singles	Single life, unexpurgated.

18

Celebs of Cyberspace

If we're to forge ahead with the creation of an "electronic democracy," as the leaders of the Electronic Frontier Foundation would have it, it's going to happen through increased communication between the world's elite and the rest of us. Sounds great, but it's easier said than done. After his e-mail address appeared in a story in *The New Yorker*, Bill Gates was inundated with messages from people he didn't know. Because of the surge, he needed help screening his e-mail. It's an unfortunate yet inevitable result of the quick and easy access e-mail offers.

The celebrities of cyberspace don't want junk mail, or flames, or random requests for advice. They don't know you, and may not even want to hear from you. But then again they might. So why not give it a try and, provided you've got something to say (that's the important part), send off some e-mail? Be courteous and try to zip off your message before the newbies inundate celebs' in-boxes with ego-stroking chatter.

To find celebrity e-mail addresses, you have two options—searching a "white pages" directory or looking for a Web page for the celebrity, if one exists. Four11 (**http://www.**

four11.com), a directory of e-mail and street addresses, includes a special link from its home page to celebrity addresses. If you don't have any luck with a visit to Four11, try a search of Yahoo! (**http://www.yahoo.com**) by entering the celebrity's name. Lots of celebs have Web pages created in their honor (often with addresses like **http://www.shaq.com**, for basketball star Shaquille O'Neal), and some of these allow you to send e-mail.

Here's a selection of the e-mail addresses of several prominent citizens of cyberspace:

Douglas Adams, author of *The Hitchhiker's Guide to the Galaxy*

adamsd@cerf.net

Scott Adams, creator of the *Dilbert* cartoon

scottadams@aol.com

John Perry Barlow, lyricist for the Grateful Dead and co-founder of the Electronic Frontier Foundation

barlow@eff.org

Nicholas Negroponte, director of the Media Lab at MIT

nicholas@media.mit.edu

Howard Rheingold, author of *Virtual Reality* and *The Virtual Community*

hlr@well.com

19

Use a :-)

If you've done time on the Internet, you've probably noticed the way the I-way's natives—the chat line and newsgroup addicts—try to add the attributes of face-to-face conversations (frowns, smiles, etc.) to their online communications. Not satisfied with words, they intersperse their missives with odd strings of standard keyboard characters. The most prevalent of these "smileys," as they're called, is the smiley face (seen as such when you tilt your head to the left):

```
:) or :-)
```

Also known as "emoticons," these conversational doodads appear all over the Net:

```
(Jerry) Got to go. Meeting someone for dinner.
(Kramer) Big date? ;-)
(Jerry) Uh uh. :-( Just a friend.
(Kramer) Have fun. =8-)
```

It's become standard, especially in chat rooms, to greet friends with a smiley, just as you would if you met a friend on the street. It lets the friend know you're happy to hear from him or her:

```
(Bart) Wuz up dude? Where u been? :-)
```

Smileys convey the body language and facial expressions missing from computer conversations. They can be used to express affection:

```
(Wilma) Have a nice day, Fred.
(Fred) Bye, honey. :-*
```

Or shock:

```
(Scotty)  Captain, we lost Dr. McCoy in the
          transporter.
(Jim) You must be joking, Scotty. 8-|
```

Or laughter:

```
(Beavis) You do your homework?
(Butthead) No. :-D :-D I forgot. :-D :-D :-D
```

A smiley can say it all:

```
(Joel) She dumped me.
(Ruth-Anne) :-(
```

New smileys appear all the time, with some rather strange ones out there.

Here's a list of commonly used smileys:

:-)	smile	%-)	up all night
:-(	frown	:-*	kiss
|-)	sleeping	=:-)	punk rocker
;-)	wink	:-o	yawn or Wow!
8-)	wearing glasses or sunglasses	:-p	sticking out tongue
		:-&	tongue-tied
,-)	one-eyed wink	(-:	left-handed smiley
:-|	bored		
;-(	crying	:-v	talking
8-|	surprised	:-c	unhappy
[]	hug	<:-|	dunce
:-D	laughing	{:)	toupee

20

Not for Women Only

In the competition for the "eyeballs" of Web viewers, sites often focus on a specific market—college students, say, or sports fans. Now, a growing number of sites target another large, and largely untapped, Internet audience: women.

Many of the best sites for women, such as the Cybergrrl Webstation (**http://www.cybergrrl.com**) and Women's Wire (**http://www.women.com**), have a vibrant, out-there spirit, offering advice, guidance, and a place to talk about everything from updating your wardrobe to making a big career move. Some sites, such as Feminist.com (**http://www.feminist.com**), have a strong political bent, while others focus on specific topics, such as film (visit Girls on Film at **http://www.girlsonfilm.com**), work (see Advancing Women at **http://www.advancing women.com**), or sports (try Just Sports for Women at **http://www.justwomen.com**).

At the Cybergrrl Webstation, you'll find everything from an interactive comic, "The Adventures of Cybergrrl," to lists of "things to read" and "places to go," while Women's

Wire, with its hip design, offers features such as "Ask Cash Flo" (financial advice) and "Heart of the Matter" (a relationships forum).

And although these sites may be designed primarily for women, that doesn't mean men won't find them interesting or useful. Consider the handy Beatrice's Web Guide (**http://www.bguide.com**), a partnership between Women's Wire and Yahoo! The site's motto? "Only the good stuff," meaning that Beatrice, a cartoon character (retro glasses, purple pants) reviews the best of what's on the Internet. It's a service of value to anyone looking for a friendly, ultra-informed guide to everything Internet. In "Ask B," Beatrice answers questions about subjects ranging from decorating a home to recent volcanic eruptions. One person, Shy Guy, asked, "How can I say to a girl in my class (I am a boy) that I like her?" Another wanted to know about quilting patterns. Beatrice obliged with helpful answers.

If you're skeptical of seeking advice from a cartoon character who prides herself on continuing in the tradition of her "virtual sisters," from Olive Oyl to Lisa Simpson, you can be assured that her answers offer useful information and links to sites where additional material can be found. Beatrice may not be a real person, but she sure knows the Net.

21

An Answer for Every Question

Of all the Internet's uses, its most valued service may be as a way to resolve long-running disputes about arcane matters, like the geographical location of the magnetic North Pole—a question I was able to answer with a few minutes of Internet sleuthing. (It's somewhere on Canada's Noice Peninsula, according to a 1994 survey explained at a Web site with an address so long and unwieldy it's not worth repeating.) Millions of documents—some reliable, some not—have been indexed by the Web's search engines, ready for you to scour for tidbits of knowledge. Conduct an intelligent search of the Web, and you may find an answer to a question you've been pondering for years.

Two friends of mine, George and Jim, have a tendency to engage in seemingly never-ending arguments about obscure topics. One protracted debate concerns the phrase, "in like Flynn." Or is it, as Jim contends, "in like Flint" (or Flynt)? George thinks Flynn, Jim thinks Flint.

As for myself, I'm an impartial observer, but after hearing the matter argued for more than two years, with no resolution, I resolved to find an answer with the help of the Internet, using the same carefully honed Internet search techniques I used to find the North Pole.

In that case, I visited the AltaVista search engine (**http://www.altavista.digital.com**) and searched for the phrase, "Where is the magnetic North Pole," putting the words in quotation marks to limit the search to the exact phrase. I got two matches, one of them being a Geological Survey of Canada site with a detailed (and reliable) explanation.

Things were not so easy when looking for Flint, Flynn, and Flynt.

Search for "in like Flynn" or "in like flint," and you'll find too many references to make sense of them. After all, what's the use of someone employing the phrase, if you don't know whether it's being used correctly? To narrow the search, I entered this query: **+"in like Flynn" +phrase**. That looked for only those pages including both the word "phrase" and the actual phrase itself, my aim being to find a page with a discussion of the Flint/Flynn/Flynt dispute. (Use the **+** sign at AltaVista when you want to ensure a certain word or phrase appears in the results of your search.)

The result? Twenty-three matches, including one for a handy site, the Word Wizard (**http://wordwizard.com**). The Word Wizard answers questions from readers, one of whom had already asked, "Is it 'in like Flynn' or 'in like Flynt?' " Flynn, according to the wizard. The phrase derives from the exploits of the actor Errol Flynn. It refers superficially "to anything speedy," and is often used "to refer to a quick and successful seduction."

That explanation was repeated, more or less, at the site for Straight Dope (**http://www.straightdope.com**), a syndicated column with answers to strange questions. Cecil Adams, the writer of Straight Dope, provides a number of sources in making the case for the Errol Flynn derivation, although he also speculates about a theory concerning a New York City political boss by the name of Flynn. Nowhere does he mention Flint or Flynt.

Of course, there's a reason why some people say "in like Flint" rather than "in like Flynn." In the 1960s, James Coburn starred in a movie, "In Like Flint," as I discovered when one of my searches turned up a reference to the flick. Hence, the confusion.

22

Going Once, Going Twice

Let's say you're looking for a speedy Pentium, but you wouldn't mind a refurbished machine, rather than a spiffy new one. You could try a catalogue retailer or the local computer store, of course, but if you want to have some fun—and engage in one of the latest cyber-experiences—think about taking a look at one of the Web's thriving auction houses.

Scores of auction houses have surfaced on the Net, allowing buyers to bid on products ranging from books to personal computers. Some sites sell used or refurbished goods, while others focus on new products. Whatever the product, the concept is the same: A minimum bid price is set, buyers submit bids from their Web browsers, and the product goes to the highest bidder once the bidding is closed.

One of the most popular online auction spots, OnSale (**http://www.onsale.com**), offers computers, peripherals, and other consumer electronics. Bidding often starts low, attracting buyers scouting the Web for a super deal, but the prices can quickly rise to those you would find at a traditional retailer. One caution, at OnSale or anywhere else: Don't let the excitement of online bidding con you into buying something for a price higher than what you would pay elsewhere.

Another site, First Auction (**http://www.firstauction. com**), functions much the same as OnSale. "Wink, blink, or even raise your hands and yell," you're informed, "but we won't take your bid until you select the price you're willing to pay and tell us how many you want!" In other words, don't fear you're going to bid high with a click of the mouse and have a monstrous 17-inch monitor delivered to your house, without realizing you bid on it.

Billed as "an auction search engine," BidFind (**http:// www.bidfind.com**) may be the most useful auction site on the Net. The site's "agent" software scans the Web's auction sites, indexing the data from them. Visit BidFind, and you can avoid surfing to lots of different auction sites. Just search for "PowerBook," "laser printer," or whatever else you want to buy, and you'll have a list of products being auctioned at sites around the Web. A search for "Pentium" turned up 439 matches.

For links to auction sites, try the Internet Auction List (**http://www.usaweb.com**). The site provides links to 1,457 auction-related sites listed in categories such as books, collectibles, heavy equipment, travel, and wine.

And if you'd like to auction something off yourself, try Haggle Online (**http://www.haggle.com**), where anyone can submit a product for bidding. A unique feature at the site allows you to view the bids previously submitted. For an IBM PC with a 386 processor, bidding started at $1. At last look, the competition had heated up, with two bidders—DM from Iselin, N.J., and DL from Fresno, Calif.—engaged in a bidding war. The price was up to $42.

23

School Days

It's your first day at college, and you're sitting on a couch in the Orientation Room, staring at photographs of the campus—the quad's broad lawns, the stately academic buildings, the football field. You're waiting for someone to tell you where you can register, but no one does. Secretaries and administrators rush through the room, not paying attention to you. After a few minutes of waiting, you notice a table with brochures and a campus map. Why not grab the map and see the campus for yourself?

You decide to skip orientation, and within a few seconds you're on the street with a few other people—some of them new, like you, but others familiar with the campus. One of them is saying hello to you, calling you by name. You wonder how she knows you, but then you remember— you're wearing a name tag. You exchange pleasantries, talk about where you're from, what bands you're into, and she asks if you want to take a walk. You say, "Sure," and you're off, exploring this unfamiliar place, thinking college might not be so bad after all.

You're not at Stanford or MIT, but at Diversity University, a virtual campus where teachers bring classes online for interactive learning sessions. A variety of classes have been held at DU, from freshman composition to basic MOO skills. Writing instructors use DU's "classrooms" to have their students converse through writing, rather than speech. Others use the space to teach workshops about navigating the Net. Running the same software as LambdaMOO (see Chapter 13), DU is a dynamic, growing place, with teachers holed up in offices and newcomers wandering the streets, meeting new friends and looking for classes to attend.

To reach Diversity University, **telnet** to **moo.du.org 8888**. After the welcome message, connect as a guest by typing **connect guest**. You'll be given a name, such as **Onyx_Guest** or **Opal_Guest**, and you'll find yourself in the Orientation Room. In typical MOO style, you'll see a description of the room:

```
Light from a number of scattered lamps and from
the Lounge to the west mix into a typical
waiting room atmosphere. A large round table
covered with brochures and folders occupies the
center of the room. Couches and chairs line the
walls which are covered with some picture-card
shots of Diversity University's campus. From
time to time you see university personnel
rushing through while trying to appear very busy
and occupied.
```

To get oriented, type **help newbie** for a list of basic commands, **help theme** for a description of the purpose of Diversity U., or **map** for a map of the campus. Before you wander too far, acquaint yourself with the etiquette of the place. Like most institutions of higher learning, DU wants to create an atmosphere conducive to its mission. Type

look manners, then **read manners**, for a brief review of what's expected of members of the university community.

"This is a communal space," the document says. "We do not tolerate offensive or hurtful behavior of any kind. Everyone's freedom ends where the freedom of others begins." It's not a free-for-all, like some MOOs. You're prohibited from creating intrusive objects or barging in on a class without permission. Moreover, administrators ask you to refrain from using sexual language or engaging in sexual acts in public.

If you're interested in exploring further—taking a class or teaching one—type **look application** for information on acquiring a character of your own. The administration recommends spending some time as a guest before requesting a permanent character. Administrators say they "need you to understand the concept (or maybe even identify with DU's cause) in order to be able to contribute to it and take advantage of its enormous potential."

At Diversity University, unlike many other MOOs, you're encouraged to use your real name as your character, with the form *Firstname_Lastname*. (I'm **Al_Hoffman** at DU.) Type **@request** to move through the application procedure. Within a few days, your character name and password will be delivered via e-mail.

Once you've got your character and password, **telnet** to the site again and connect by typing **connect** *character_name password*. You'll find yourself in the Student Union Center, with "an old red couch in the corner, usually occupied by sleeping students." You can wander around, of course, meeting other students, but you might want to head to the Registration Hall to find out about the courses being offered at DU.

To get to the registration area, head east (type **east**) to the Administration Hall, leaving "the noisy Student Union

---

103

Center," and then walk further east (again, type **east**, or **e**) to the Administration Building, an edifice looking like it was "designed to intimidate incoming freshmen with its immensity and grandeur." Now move **south** to the Registration Hall, where you'll find directions for entering other rooms for information on classes.

If you get lost, type **look** to see where you are. Typing **@ways** will provide a list of exits; typing **@go student** will return you to the Student Union Center. And you can always talk to someone nearby by typing a quotation mark, followed by what you want to say. If you want to say, "I'm lost," type **"I'm lost."** On your screen, you'll see the following:

```
You say, "I'm lost."
```

Others in the room or the street would see the name of your character—Garnet_Guest, say—followed by your words:

```
Garnet_Guest says, "I'm lost."
```

If you're lucky, someone will offer help. To leave the university, type **@quit**.

24

Advice from an Agent

If it's up to a number of Web sites, such as Microsoft Expedia, Travelocity and 1travel.com, you'll soon be thinking of a "travel agent" as a computer program searching for hot deals, rather than a friendly person helping you select destinations and arrange travel plans. "Agent" software is being used on the Web to translate an individual's personal preferences and desires—a midweek flight to San Diego, say—into intelligent, timely, and cost-saving information.

Think of a software agent as a personal helper. You tell the agent what you're hoping to find, and it will search for that information, reporting back to you when it finds it. Consider the Fare Watcher Email service by Travelocity (**http://www.travelocity.com**). Once you register for the free service, you're able to select several round-trip routes for your software agent to track. Any time an airline fare changes by $25 or more on one of those routes, you're notified by e-mail. Another service, 1travel.com (**http://www.1travel.com**), offers similar help, notifying you when special deals match your preferences. In addition, 1travel.com will set up a Web page providing the details on matching offers. A Microsoft site, Expedia (**http://www.expedia. com**), includes a Fare Tracker service to keep you up-to-date on the best airline deals. After you register, you select three trips, and Expedia will send you a weekly e-mail with the best deals for those routes.

Other travel sites simply compile the best deals. At WebFlyer (**http://www.insideflyer.com**), the motto is "It's all about miles"—an apt description of the site, given its emphasis on special deals and frequent flyer miles. One area of WebFlyer compiles the best deals each week on flights, hotels, and car rentals. American Express Travel (**http://www.americanexpress.com/travel/**) does much the same, offering a section with last-minute travel deals in categories such as flights, cruises, and vacations.

Of course, it's one thing to visit a Web page for information on cheap fares, and another thing to have your agent inform you when a deal is available. Agents—also called "bots" (as in "robot")—can save you time and money. And they're capable of doing more, much more, than look for the best deals for airline flights.

The agent software at Firefly (**http://www.firefly.com**) will serve as an entertainment adviser, recommending movies and music based on your ratings of films and bands. (Let's say you like Joe Henry and the Replacements. If someone else likes those artists, plus another—Cake, say—then Firefly recommends Cake.) At the Monster Board (**http://www.monster.com**), one of the Web's most popular career sites, a "personal job search agent" will scope out positions you might want. And AutoAgent—available at AutoWeb Interactive (**http://www.autoweb.com**)—will let you know when the used vehicle of your choice is available. For assistance from other agents, visit BotSpot (**http://www.botspot.com**), a clearinghouse of agent sites on the Net.

25

Deep in the Heart
of MUDville

Hundreds of MUDs exist on the Net, but it's not always easy to find one open for business and willing to accept you as a guest. Short for Multi-User Dungeon (or Dimension), MUDs rank among the coolest, most inventive places in cyberspace. Unfortunately, they're not among the most accessible. Often run by college students, sometimes on "borrowed" disk space at university computers, these experiments in virtual reality don't always have the same names, Net addresses, or administrators as they did last week.

Some MUDs have limits on the number of players they accept. Others have rules so complex it makes learning difficult for a newbie—that is, unless you've got a 19-year-old buddy and MUDhacker willing to guide you through the arcane rules governing hexes and curses.

Expect to do some exploring before you find the right MUD—one without a whole lot of killing, say (some devote themselves to such activities), but with lots of hobbits and elves. Connecting to a MUD can be a daunting task, yet it's one with great rewards, especially if you're interested in exploring worlds at the dark edges of fantasy and science fiction.

For an introduction to MUDs, along with information on how (and where) to get involved in them, visit the Mud Connector (**http://www.mudconnect.com**), a site with a simple introduction for MUD newbies. The Mud Connector allows you to search through MUDs by name or type. Even if you're not interested in engaging in an Internet version of Dungeons and Dragons, don't dismiss a visit altogether; some of the more sophisticated MUDs shun the game paradigm and offer a world where the inhabitants don't compete so much as hang out, experiencing what it's like to invent and occupy a collaboratively imagined world.

The Mud Connector lists hundreds of MUDs, from Arcane Nites (**http://mud.pht.com/~mud/**), a MUD populated with werewolves and vampires, to Adventures for Ancient Wisdom (**http://score.ton.tut.fi/~mud/**), a site with "a specially built newbie-friendly mud school."

The Web pages for MUDs often have instructions on joining, along with profiles of regulars and a description of the MUD to give you a sense of whether it's to your liking. Click the "connect" link and your PC, if configured to do so, will launch **telnet** to connect to the MUD.

Visit RockyMud (**http://www.divide.com/rocky/**), for instance, and you'll find yourself at a page with the self-proclaimed aim of trying to "brainwash others into joining us." RockyMud boasts of having one of the "nicest groups of players you could ever meet." Like a "family," the site claims: "A strange violent freakish one, but a family nonetheless." A family, through something called a MUD? If you're willing to enter a virtual world, that's what you may find—even if it's a family of odd creatures, with few humans in sight.

If you have trouble connecting to a MUD, it's probably because the MUD is out of commission, has moved, or you're trying to connect at a time when the wizards—the powerful folks who "build" these virtual worlds—are constructing new challenges for lowly MUD wanderers like yourself. Try again at another time, or try another MUD.

For more information on MUDs and other M-worlds (MOOs, MUCKs, and so on), head to these newsgroups:

alt.mud	assorted MUD info
rec.games.mud.admin	the administrative side of MUDs
rec.games.mud.announce	announcements about MUDs
rec.games.mud.diku	devoted to DikuMUDs, a popular type of MUD
rec.games.mud.lp	devoted to the most common type of MUDs, LPMUDs
rec.games.mud.misc	miscellaneous MUD postings
rec.games.mud.tiny	devoted to the Tiny family of MUDs

26

You Don't
Know What?

The categories say it all: "Origin of the Comic Species," "Bad British Accountants," "A Pox Upon Ye," "Measure This!" and "Secretaries of the World, Unite!" If you're looking for a quiz show with attitude, look no further than "You Don't Know Jack," the popular CD-ROM game that's now available on the Net.

You can play lots of games over the Net, from simple ones, like tic-tac-toe, to outrageously elaborate creations—the role-playing games called MUDs come to mind—but few offer the immersive, in-your-face experience of "You Don't Know Jack." Like other sites offering over-the-Internet games, such as Playsite (**http://www.playsite. com**), "You Don't Know Jack" aims to bring Net gaming to the masses. It's billed as "the show where high culture and pop culture collide."

To play "You Don't Know Jack" requires a separate application available at **http://www.bezerk.com**. (Installation instructions are provided at the site.) After downloading the free software, you can participate in twice-weekly quiz shows. Once you launch "Jack" on your PC—

be sure you're connected to the Net—a new game will be downloaded in the background as the announcer asks you to enter your name and the number of players (two can compete at one time).

From the start of "Jack," you know you're not in the land of *Jeopardy!* This is a quiz show with an announcer who's a lot more like Jim Carrey than Alex Trebek. Don't expect polite responses when you get a question wrong. In fact, you should be prepared for a few wisecracks. Like a lot of CD-ROMs, the game seems to take control of your computer screen, making for an experience that's a lot more TV-like than most of what you view on the Net. Commercials for companies such as Budweiser and Yahoo! appear at the start of the game and in between questions. Music blasts from your speakers. Questions zip from one end of your screen to the other. Playing "Jack," you don't have the sense of being on the Net so much as starring in your own TV show.

As for the questions themselves, they're often challenging, requiring a knowledge of everything from Shakespeare to Motley Crüe. One question asked what stud maintains the sex act the longest (humans prevailed over chimps and horses). Another wanted to know what TV show rhymes with the phrase, "Trevor rebills. I know to run slow." I would have gotten the answer, but the announcer kept shouting at me—he's intentionally obnoxious—and that led to a few too many typos. The answer: "Beverly Hills 90210."

In contrast to the Generation-X feel of "You Don't Know Jack," Playsite offers something a lot more traditional—although no less compelling in its technology. Rather than requiring you to install a separate application on your hard drive, Playsite uses the Java programming language for its versions of chess, checkers, and backgammon. Once you've got Playsite running on your PC, you can play games with people halfway around the globe. Not only that, you can chat with them during the games.

And this, you can be sure, is only the beginning. With so much interest in Net gaming, you can expect these games to metamorphose into mega-shows for the new millennium.

27

Stopping by the
Software Storehouse

The next time you're looking for a new computer program, whether you want an adventure game or a simple spreadsheet, think about searching the Web before scanning the shelves of a computer superstore. The Web offers access to thousands of free, or nearly free, software titles, commonly known as shareware. The creators of these programs generally ask for a fee—anywhere from a few dollars on up—if you keep the program, but some programmers simply give away their handiwork, asking only for an e-mail message ("Thanks! Love the program!") or a postcard ("Greetings from Hoboken!").

Just a few years ago, in the Jurassic Age of the Internet, finding shareware was not a simple task. It required the use of obscure-looking commands, and even then it was hard to know whether a program was reliable or worth using. Things have changed. A number of Web sites have streamlined the process of searching for software on the Web, making it simple to find programs and download them.

Shareware.com (**http://www.shareware.com**) excels in providing a swift search mechanism to find software. Enter a keyword or two (**music**, say, or **iq test**), the type of computer system you've got (the options include Windows, Macintosh, and several others, such as Atari and Amiga), and soon you'll have a list of programs. If you want one of them, Shareware.com connects you to sites where you can download the program and provides an estimate of the download time.

Just the other day, I needed a program for my Macintosh to create a flow chart. I didn't want to buy one—I knew I'd only use it a few times—but I was able to pick up DesignerDraw, a program more than adequate for my needs, within five minutes. And the price was right, too. The program's creator, Paul Hyman, gives it away for free, asking only for comments from users.

One of the most valuable areas of Shareware.com offers editors' recommendations for the best titles for Windows and Macintosh computers in different categories, such as business, education and kids. The selection of games includes the Windows program Marble ($10), described as "elegantly simple and maddeningly difficult," and the Macintosh game Giza ($15), a first-person adventure game.

Like Shareware.com, the ZDNet Software Library (**http://www.hotfiles.com**) allows you to search for files and download them, but the site's real strength is in from its recommendations and editorial features—not surprising, given that the site was created by the publishers of *PC Week*, *PC Computing*, and other computer magazines. The site's "toolkits" gather software to use for specific purposes. A toolkit for road trips included shareware to help you plan a route, decide where to stay, and organize your photos. Other highlights of the site include the Hot File of the Day and discussion areas devoted to talk about software, such as the ZD Shareware Game-of-the-Year, Duke Nukem 3D (topics include "Is Doom Dead?" and "Which has better weapons—Duke or Quake?").

Jumbo (**http://www.jumbo.com**), another shareware site, offers access to more than 200,000 programs, dividing them into 15 subject areas, such as desktop publishing, education, and multimedia. The programs run the gamut from SAT tutors to shoot-'em-up games.

The programs available at these sites may not replace your most reliable and trusted software, but they're likely to help you have some fun or make your work a bit easier.

28

The Classics, Online

Most people would still rather settle in with a well-worn copy of *Uncle Tom's Cabin* or *Emma* than read it on a computer screen, but that hasn't stopped the advocates of electronic texts from moving forward with efforts to bring literature to the digital world. It's now possible to read everything from *Paradise Lost* to *The Call of the Wild* online, forgoing a trip to the library—the "physical" library, that is—or the bookstore. These works may not look very attractive on the screen, and most of them don't offer the convenience of their print counterparts—you can't flip through pages as easily on the Web as you can with a book—but they do offer quick, cheap, and easy access to enduring works of literature.

Project Gutenberg (**http://www.promo.net/pg/**), the pioneering effort to create electronic versions of print works, continues to offer hundreds of electronic texts. Begun 25 years ago with the aim of converting 10,000 texts to electronic format, the project hasn't met its goal yet, but it remains a useful resource, offering everything from the Declaration of Independence and the Bill of Rights—two of the first texts added to its archive—to Zane Grey's *The*

Redheaded Outfield and Elizabeth Gaskell's *Cranford*. Unfortunately, the formatting of many of these texts leaves much to be desired. Most people would find reading more than a couple of pages rough going.

Other sites have gone further in presenting books in ways to make reading online a more pleasurable experience. *The Complete Works of William Shakespeare* (**http://the-tech.mit.edu/Shakespeare/works.html**) offers a wonderful means of accessing his plays and poetry. Rather than dumping the text online, the site separates each play into scenes and allows you to click on selected words to gain access to a glossary. A search function allows you to search for words appearing in all of his works, or just in selected ones. In a discussion area, the topics include "Who is Shakespeare's greatest villain?" and "Herbs and flowers in Shakespeare."

Another resource, the Bartleby Library at Columbia University (**http://www.columbia.edu/acis/bartleby/**), offers a diverse selection of texts, including Agatha Christie's *The Mysterious Affair at Styles*, Thomas Paine's *Common Sense*, and Mary Wollstonecraft's *Vindication of the Rights of Woman*. Like the Shakespeare site, Bartleby's texts have been designed with viewing on the Web in mind.

For a clearinghouse with links to texts across the Web, try the On-line Books Page (**http://www.cs.cmu.edu/books.html**). The site classifies books alphabetically and by subject. It also indicates whether the work appears as a plain text file or as a document designed for presentation on the Web. You'll find a great variety of books at the site, both well-known ones, including Willa Cather's *My Antonia*, and more obscure works, such as *Where Pigeons Go to Die* by R. Wright Campbell.

29

Your Own Arcade

Snowboarding may not be your sport of choice, but don't let that stop you from taking a whirl on the slopes. With Extreme Snowboarding (**http://eriver1.com/arcade/snoboard.html**), a game available on the Web, you'll be careening down a mountain in no time, jumping over rocks and aiming for the finish line. The game, produced by Eagle River Interactive, puts you on a slalom snowboarding course with red and blue gates and mountains in the distance. You're represented by a gnarly kid with a mohawk, and as you zoom down the slopes, navigating with your mouse, you hear the sound of the snow and ice underneath your board.

The game offers different levels—easy, hard and expert—and requires skill and practice, especially if you don't want to get tossed into the air by a rock. The first time I played, I jumped a rock or two, but I also ran into quite a few trees. (Apparently, it's not possible to get injured in Extreme Snowboarding.) The game feels so real, with the mohawked kid sliding over the snow and the mountains changing perspective in the background, you might even get dizzy.

Extreme Snowboarding, like many games you can play directly in the window of your Web browser, makes use of a technology called Shockwave to bring sound and action to the Web experience. To play these games, you should be using the latest version of either Netscape Navigator or Internet Explorer, and you must install the Shockwave plug-in from Macromedia's Shockwave Download Center at **http://www.macromedia.com/shockwave/download/ index.cgi** (see Chapter 9 for details on plug-ins).

If you're not ready for winter sports, then try a more traditional arcade-style game. A number of game developers have adapted classic arcade and computer games for the Web. Saturday!, a multimedia consulting firm, features Web versions of Tetris and Asteroids. Quatris (**http://www.imperium.net/~onedan/Saturday/games/ quatris.html**), called a "dropping-shape game" by its creator, Dan Berlyoung of Akron, Ohio, is simple and easy to play—and a quick download, too—as is 'Stroids (**http:// www.imperium.net/~onedan/Saturday/games/stroids. html**).

For something on the strange side, try Broderbund's Mudball Wall (**http://www.broderbund.com/studio/ activemind/mudball.html**). You've got to see it to believe it, but the game basically involves a simple concept— constructing mudballs and hurling them against a wall. The wacky design makes it all worthwhile, even if it seems a bit pointless. You can decide on the color of your mud balls, and also choose their shapes, selecting from a star, triangle, diamond, circle, and square. The site has great sound effects. As the Mudball Launcher winds up, you hear it creaking. The mud splats as it hits the wall.

For children, there's Mello Smello Games & Coloring Books (**http://www.mellosmello.com/games/index.html**), a site with a series of easy-to-play Shockwave games. One game, What's Different, presents two pictures, each a slight variation of the other. Click on the piece that's different (an extra cloud, say, or a pterodactyl), and you score a point. Another game asks, "Can You Find the 10 Things Wrong with This Picture?" I tried. For starters, there was the egg with the zipper, the dinosaur with two heads, and the tree with the "For Sale" sign.

Other games worth checking out include Web Frog and Web Invaders, both available at AfterShock (**http://www.ashock.com/html/arcadealley.html**), and Braniac Interactive Group's Headball (**http://www.brainiactive.com/headball.html**), an offbeat game involving hitting a person's head across a court.

These games might not be Doom or Quake, but they're a fun diversion.

30

....

All the Jargon
That's Fit to Print

....

After a few weeks of exploring the Net, you're bound to have a friend accuse you of retreating from the "real world" and descending into the Stygian depths of computer geekdom. You'll be telling this friend about the great GIFs you found, or about a cool newsgroup called **alt.folklore. urban**, and he'll give you a strange look and say, "You're a hacker."

"Huh?" you respond.

"A hacker. You know, one of those computer freaks."

You, a hacker? You don't think of yourself as a hacker. You're just interested in all this cool stuff you're finding on the Net. What's wrong with that? And what is a *hacker*, anyhow? Is it in the dictionary? You could look it up in Webster's, but why not see if you can find a definition on the Net. Could he be right? Could you, *normal* you, be a hacker?

The Jargon File **(http://www.ccil.org/jargon/)**, a dictionary of hacker slang, defines hacker as follows:

```
hacker: [originally, someone who makes furniture
with an axe] n.

1. A person who enjoys exploring the details of
programmable systems and how to stretch their
capabilities, as opposed to most users, who
prefer to learn only the minimum necessary.
2. One who programs enthusiastically (even
obsessively) or who enjoys programming rather
than just theorizing about programming.
```

Whether or not you qualify as a hacker, you may come across hackish words in your travels on the Net, and it helps to know them. You'll find a trove of jargon in this dictionary of hacker slang. The Jargon File covers "the language hackers use among themselves for fun, social communication, and technical debate."

Aside from the Jargon File—now in print as *The New Hacker's Dictionary*—a number of Web references, such as Netdictionary, (**http://www.netdictionary.com**), NetLingo (**http://www.netlingo.com**), and Whatis.com (**http://what is.com**), will help you "upgrade" your Internet vocabulary.

No matter how techno-literate you may be, you're certain to come across acronyms and buzzwords you don't know: *ADSL. Bots. Shockwave.* It's not necessary to know these words to e-mail friends or surf the Net, but it helps. When a Web site offers a personal "agent" to help you choose a travel destination, or your Internet service provider sends you a brochure about ISDN, it doesn't hurt if you understand the terminology.

For its simple interface and comprehensive list of terms, visit Whatis.com when you're suffering from acronym overload. You've always wondered what "AI" means? Select the link at Whatis.com, and there's a definition: "The simulation of human intelligence processes by machines, especially computer systems." Like other Internet glossaries, Whatis.com offers links between definitions. The definition of AI provides a link to "expert system," a type of program that "simulates the judgment and behavior of a human or an organization that has expert knowledge and experience in a particular field." Follow the links from one definition to another, and soon you'll be well on your way to acquiring the vocabulary of a hacker.

31

On the Road

If you're planning a trip, you might want to consider soliciting advice from a cyberjock or two. In the age of the electrosphere, you're just a few keystrokes away from the idiosyncratic recommendations of people who know everything about the biking in Brisbane, the inns in Vancouver, and the mud baths in the Badlands. The various **rec.travel** Usenet groups—**rec.travel.air**, **rec.travel.asia**, **rec.travel. cruises**, **rec.travel.europe**, **rec.travel.marketplace**, **rec. travel.misc**, and **rec.travel.usa-canada**—allow Netheads to share information on every travel-related topic from all-purpose soap to extravagant island vacations. You can try to find a driving partner, request a list of hot spots in a specific locale, or ask for hotel recommendations.

These newsgroups are the sort of cyberspace hangouts that make budding infonauts wild about the Net. Take a trip through a **rec.travel** group, and you will tap into a vast body of knowledge about where your fellow info-travelers live and where they've been. Sitting at your desk, contemplating a computer-free trip to the peaks of the Alps or the beaches of Maui, you can connect with people across the world in ways that would otherwise have been impossible.

Take the guy who was looking for a honeymoon destination. Two weeks after posting a message asking for suggestions, he had 11 responses, most of them with the sort of personal details you wouldn't get in a traditional travel guide. Some came from people on tight budgets, others from those with money to blow. Some put a premium on romance, others on adventure. The suggestions ranged from Cape Elizabeth, Maine ("Get one of the beach cottages"), and Provincetown ("To truly enjoy P-town, you must have a fairly liberal outlook") to Corsica ("You can be on the beach in the morning and hiking in the mountains in the afternoon") and Bora Bora ("You have your own bungalow that sits over the water in the lagoon, with the fishes swimming right up to your glass-bottom coffee table"). If you want to hear more, you can always send e-mail.

Quite a few people use the **rec.travel** groups to find companions for their trips. Here's someone seeking a cross-country driving partner:

```
I'll be driving West to East (San Diego-D.C.)
and all my friends are wimps who want to fly. I
am looking for a person to join me to share
driving time (automatic transmission) and gas
money. I have a great reliable car with CD
player...E-mail me if interested.
```

Others ask for hints from the locals:

```
At the end of June I will be in the Pompano
Beach/Fort Lauderdale area and truly love good
fresh seafood. No, I am not looking for a chain
such as Red Lobster. Can anyone recommend a good
local place with great food, super atmosphere,
and reasonable prices???
```

But the topics range far and wide, just like the potential destinations:

```
FAQ for Seattle, Washington, USA
Travelling in Australia?
Driving (on the wrong side)
Looking for advice on travel to Turkey
Things to do in Portugal?
Wings of the World Airline, Any Feedback?
Thailand Ripoffs
Passports...how quickly?
Help with Hostels!?!!
Does this place exist?
```

Sure, you have to check things out—don't simply assume all the info's reliable—but it certainly beats getting bland brochures from the chamber of commerce and the bureau of tourism. People on the Net speak bluntly and directly. One person posted a message saying he'd made reservations at a camper village near the Grand Canyon; he wanted to know what to expect. "It's nearly wall-to-wall RVs, and many run their generators early and late to watch TV," he was told. Someone else, who used to work near the camper village, agreed: "Expect to hear helicopters," he said. "It's close to a base for copter touring companies." He recommended the Kaibab National Forest, also near the Grand Canyon, for back-country camping. He offered detailed directions, complete with route numbers and landmarks ("the abandoned fire tower on the east side of the highway"), to a perfect, remote spot.

Post a message to **rec.travel.usa-canada**, and you may even have people telling you what to do, even if it doesn't fit your plans. A woman looking for info on parking a rental car outside of Manhattan got this response:

```
Why do you want a car at all there? It will do you
very little good and be a source of great hassle.
Take the bus from Newark Airport into Manhattan,
and get around by bus, subway, and foot. When
you're ready to leave the greater NYC area, *that*
might be the right time to rent a car.
```

Yet for every infonaut trying to run your life, you'll find 10 others with useful advice. In this case, another Net helper offered information on parking in Jersey City and taking the PATH train into Manhattan. He included costs, mileages, different options—it was like having a personal travel consultant or a highly conscientious friend, someone concerned for your safety and well-being.

If you can't find what you want on the **rec.travel** newsgroups, consider hopping over to the Rec.Travel Library at **http://www.travel-library.com**. The site offers tips, advice and guidebooks from fellow travelers. The travelogues range from "Jenny's Views of Bangkok" and "Greece: Cycling in the Lap of the Gods" to "Strange But True Southwest" and "Two Wheels, Three Fins, Four Brits, and Five Days in Java." And if you want to share some of your own travel experiences, the site always welcomes fresh contributions.

32

Surfing the City

It's Friday night, and you're planning the next day's jaunt into the city. Do you want to see the Cindy Sherman exhibit at the Museum of Modern Art? Or visit a gallery in Chelsea and have dinner at a sushi joint? If you need assistance in making a selection, the Web's got a number of sites to help you decide what to do with your weekend.

In an area of keen competition on the Web, a number of "city guides" aim to serve as your personal resource for all things urban, especially when it comes to arts and entertainment listings. The most high-profile ventures, City-Search (**http://www.citysearch.com**) and Sidewalk (**http://www.sidewalk.com**)—the former a start-up venture, the latter a Microsoft operation—have sites in several cities already, with more in the works. Whether you're looking for a restaurant or a reading, these sites want you to turn to them for guidance.

The concept is a simple one: You're looking for something to do in Manhattan, say, and rather than flipping through *New York* magazine or the *Village Voice*, you log onto the Web and either enter a keyword ("road race," say, or "country music") or scan the categories of listings: art galleries, bars, books and talks, dance, kids and family, music, restaurants. If something's happening—and something always is—it's likely to be listed in one of the site's Web databases. On the day I visited the CitySearch site for New York, 2,945 events were listed, with 71 sites added that day alone.

One of the more useful features of CitySearch—and one that's available, in a slightly different form, at Sidewalk—allows you to customize the site to send you periodic e-mail messages about events you might want to attend. (Registration is necessary for this feature. It's free and painless.) Tell CitySearch you're a fan of John Hiatt or Wilco, and they'll send you a message when there's an upcoming performance. Or, if you'd like a selection of the week's top picks, CitySearch will send you a weekly e-mail in any number of categories, including books and classical music.

Other sites, such as City.Net (**http://www.city.net**), Digital City (**http://www.digitalcity.com**), and the Yahoo! series of city guides (**http://www.yahoo.com**), offer some of the same services as CitySearch and Sidewalk, but they don't go nearly as far as those sites in providing extensive databases of listings and original recommendations and reviews. With these sites as your guide, you'll never be able to say there's nothing to do.

33

The Museum,
Via Your Mouse

To view the major works of art at the Louvre—
da Vinci's *Mona Lisa*, the *Venus de Milo*, Vermeer's *The Astronomer*—you no longer have to walk miles from the Richelieu wing to the Denon wing, much less fly to France. At the museum's Web site (**http://www.louvre.fr**), it takes just a few clicks of the mouse, and no steps at all, to move from a room with Greek antiquities to one with paintings by the Dutch masters. Like other museums on the Web, the Louvre does not make its entire collection available online, but presents highlights, along with information on visiting hours, cultural activities and future projects. By combining images of paintings, sculptures, and other *objets d'art* from the museum's collections with historical background on the Louvre itself, the site creates a rich and enlightening, if wholly virtual, experience.

While no one who loves viewing art in museums would suggest substituting a virtual visit for a real one, the virtual exhibits do have their advantages. On the Web, you don't have to worry about crowds or cramming your visit into an afternoon, and you can visit whenever you've got the time—before breakfast, during your lunch break or post-*Seinfeld*. The best online exhibits, such as the one for a popular Cezanne show at the Philadelphia Museum of Art (**http://pma.libertynet.org**), excel at transforming the browsing experience into an educational one. The site created for the Cezanne show presented a selection of Cezanne's masterpieces, such as *The Large Bathers* and *The Pont de Maincy*, along with lucid commentary accompanying the paintings. The online version of the exhibit served as a worthy complement to the actual exhibit, providing access to background materials and other resources not available at the museum itself.

Hundreds of museums have Web sites, with some of them offering large selections of art, others offering only a painting or two, and some presenting special Web-only features. The site for the Museum of Modern Art (**http://www.moma.org**) includes a series of Web projects, such as "Mutant Materials in Contemporary Design," while the Andy Warhol Museum (**http://www.warhol.org/warhol**) includes a tour through the museum, with samples of Warhol's art along the way. Others museums worth a virtual visit include the Los Angeles County Museum of Art (**http://www.lacma.org**), the Metropolitan Museum of Art (**http://www.metmuseum.org**), and the Museum of Fine Arts in Boston (**http://www.mfa.org**).

For a list of museums on the Web, visit either World Wide Arts Resources (**http://www.wwar.com**) or the Guide to Museums and Cultural Resources (**http://www.lam.mus.ca.us/webmuseums/**).

34

....

Your John Hancock

....

A signature can say a lot about a person. If it's raucous and wildly unintelligible, the smeared blue ink careening off the page, you're likely to envision its owner as a person with a messy desk, caffeine overload and an overflowing appointment book. If the signature is diminutive and careful, you imagine someone with a shy, self-effacing personality.

Unfortunately, when you send e-mail or post to a newsgroup, you can't include the intensely personal flourish of an inked signature (not yet, anyhow). Communication by computer is often extraordinarily impersonal. Yet it doesn't need to be. The cybercowboys who've settled the electronic frontier have devised ingenious ways to bring the idio-syncracies of more traditional correspondence to electronic communications. One of the more ubiquitous methods is through the use of an electronic signature.

Most Internet service providers offer a way to person-alize your online communications with a signature. The recipients of your postings and e-mail messages won't get a graphic image of your "real" signature, but they will get a personally crafted computer design, one all your own, constructed from the characters on your keyboard. Once you create such a signature, it will be appended to your communications.

Signatures vary from the understated to the elaborate. Most often, they're used as simple tags for messages—a way to inform others about the person lurking behind an obscure e-mail address. Mine is rather simple:

```
--
Allan Hoffman              author of 50 FUN
alh@web100.com                WAYS TO INTERNET
```

Yet a signature can also be used to add a graphic element to online communications. If I were to use a more complex signature, it might look something like this:

```
%%%%%%      %%        "We are in great haste to
%      %     %%        construct a magnetic
%      %     %%        telegraph from Maine to
%%%%%%      %%        Texas; but Maine and Texas,
%      %     %%        it may be, have nothing
%      %     %%        important to communicate."
%      %     %%%%%%            Henry David Thoreau

                            Allan Hoffman
                            alh@web100.com

                      author of 50 FUN WAYS TO
                            INTERNET
```

But the preference, especially among those who frequent the Net, is for brief signatures—four lines or less. It gets tiresome, and downright annoying, for newsgroup and mailing list regulars to scroll through the same two-screen signature, full of quotations from Ray Bradbury and nifty designs, again and again and again. If that's your schtick, ply your trade in the **alt.ascii-art** newsgroup.

Different e-mail programs and newsreaders have different means of creating signatures, but most entail creating a file containing the text you want to use as your signature. Be sure to use a monospaced font to compose your signature. Such a font devotes the same amount of space to each character, whether the character is a capital M or a lowercase i. Use the standard characters on your keyboard and add spaces with the space bar, rather than with tabs. For ideas on how to make the most of the numbers, letters and other squiggly things on your keyboard, check out **alt.ascii-art**. Just don't overdo it.

However you design your signature, remember to include only information you'd like all recipients to receive, such as your e-mail address. Many people also include quotations ("Our life is frittered away by detail. Simplify, simplify.") and disclaimers ("These musings reflect my warped thoughts and not my employer's"). While an electronic signature may not have the personal flourish of the real thing, it is an opportunity to set your online communications apart from everyone else's.

35

The White House,
Online

Wondering what's up at the White House? Feel like reading the text of the president's proclamation on Older Americans Month? How about a transcript of his remarks to the Association for a Better New York? Or maybe you want to see a photograph of the president and his family. If you're interested in the goings-on at the White House, you're in luck. The Clinton administration not only supports the I-Way, it's got a full-fledged—and growing—stop on the Internet. Using e-mail or the World Wide Web, you can tour the White House and obtain copies of all types of government documents—everything from the federal budget (make sure you've got enough space on your hard drive) to transcripts of just about everything the president says, whether it's the State of the Union address or a few remarks to the American Nurses Association. You can even get a copy of President Clinton's public schedule.

The Web is certainly the most colorful and engaging way to visit the White House. To visit via the Web, point your browser to **http://www.whitehouse.gov/**, where you'll find yourself looking at a color photograph of the

White House—the gateway to a site labeled the "Interactive Citizens' Handbook." It's a well-designed spot, with lots of photographs and useful links to government information. You'll find links for the vice president's favorite political cartoons, the Hillary Rodham Clinton home page, a tour of the White House and a map of Washington, D.C., among other things. If you've got an audio-savvy computer, you can even hear greetings from the president and vice president.

E-mail may not be as exciting as a Web site with photos and audio clips, but it's a quick way to retrieve documents from the White House. To use e-mail to get a White House document, begin by searching for information on a specific topic. To do this, simply send an e-mail message to **publications@whitehouse.gov** with a line of the form **topic** *string* in the body of the message. The White House's automatic mail response system will send you information, if any, on the relevant files.

Let's say you send a message to the White House with the string **topic sex**. Will you get admonitions about safe sex, or what? You'll probably get the following, and not much else:

```
Matching Filenames:
---------------------
File-# Name
215056 pub/political-science/whitehouse-
papers/1993/Jan/STATEMENT-OF-DEPARTMENT-OF-
DEFENSE-POLICY-REGARDING-HOMOSEXUALS (3019 bytes)
```

With the file number corresponding to the document—215056 for the file above—you can retrieve the document with another e-mail message. Send the message to **publications@whitehouse.gov**, with **sendfile** *file_number* in the body of the message. To get the statement on homosexuals in the military, send the message **sendfile 215056**. With a speedy e-mail system, you'll get the statement in less than a minute.

For more details on how to get White House publications, send a message with the word **hello** in the subject line to **publications@pub.pub.whitehouse.gov**.

36

Author, Author

It's not clear who, if anyone, reads the poems in the **rec.arts.poems** Usenet newsgroup, yet thousands of poets post their work each month. You've got poems about driving at night ("The world drifts past, / Blurred, land indistinguishable") and weeds ("I cannot / will not destroy them / just because I did not invite them / to grow"). You've got poems about lost socks ("I wonder if it's lonely") and their travails ("The other socks are all in pairs / And this one's unattached / I hope it's not too painful / Being condemned to stay unmatched"). If you're in need of a poem, you can even request one: "Marry Me poem wanted." Some newsgroups function as sites for discussion of issues, but not **rec.arts.poems**. This newsgroup serves mainly as a place for poets to publish their work.

Publish, you say? Is that publishing?

Just what it means to publish is a concept being challenged by the ways of the online world. The cybersphere's most fervent denizens see the Net as democratizing the publishing industry. With its ability to allow an individual to reach millions of others, the Net circumvents the elite and insular world of the mainstream media, they say. Not everyone agrees. Others say the mass media play a useful and necessary role in discriminating among what's exceptional, what's mediocre and what's very, very bad. After all, who wants to sift through a lot of unfiltered dreck?

It's an argument at the heart of discussions about what the Net will become and where it's headed. Will it eliminate the need for the "gatekeepers" of the media, putting the power in the hands of the people, or will it mean we'll need more and more "information experts" to handle the onslaught of words and images?

Such issues may not get discussed in newsgroups set up to publish and share poetry and prose, but they're not far from the surface. A newsgroup like **rec.arts.poems**, where anyone can post any poem, represents the Net at its most open and unfiltered extreme. No editors. No cash. Just poems. For the aspiring poet, especially for one who's far from the poetry slams of New York and L.A., it's a way to share your work and read the work of others—and maybe get a response.

Other groups where you can publish your writing on the Internet include **alt.books.reviews** and **rec.arts.prose**. Neither reports the volume of **rec.arts.poems**, but both can be expected to grow. And if you want readers, lots of them, **alt.sex.stories** is the place. It's one of Usenet's most active newsgroups, with postings like these:

```
HOME IMPROVEMENT: Hot Tub Hijinks
STORY: Soft Comfort
Anyone ever get stuck in mud?
Hunk (bisexual)
ARCHIVE: road-trip
WANTED: THE MOST HORNY STORY EVER
A Prom Twist
```

Certainly it's not for everyone.

37

....

Write to a
Letter-Writer

....

Interactivity. It's one of the buzzwords of the information highway, yet no one's quite sure what it means. Is a telephone call interactive? Is electronic mail? What about an online chat? Or is the future of interactivity in a new machine, a hybrid of the personal computer and the television (and maybe the telephone), with a remote control allowing you to do everything from participate in a TV sitcom to renew your automobile registration? Some visionaries would like to see all of that, but we're not there yet, and as you contemplate such scenarios, you may as well use what interactivity you've got.

Major national publications, from *Rolling Stone* to *Wired*, have decided they want to offer some level of interactivity to their readers, and, like other institutions trying to figure out what interactivity means, they're experimenting with the myriad of possibilities presented by the nascent interactive world. *Wired*, a slick magazine with a focus on technology and the future, has gone further than any other publication in bringing interactivity to the masses. The magazine has e-mail addresses for everything from ad sales to editorial guidelines to orders for Wired Ware (T-shirts and other products), and it offers access to the magazine through its HotWired site on the Web at **http://www.hotwired.com**.

One of the simplest ways to ease yourself into the world of interactivity is to send e-mail to a letter-writer. It may be low-tech, as far as interactivity goes, but it's available now, and that's something. Both *Rolling Stone* and *Wired*, among many other publications, receive letters by e-mail. Pick up one of those magazines, and you're bound to see an Internet address below a letter-writer's name. This allows you to do something you probably wouldn't have done otherwise—respond directly to that person, a fellow reader and cyberjock. You can vent your frustration or anger, or maybe express your empathy with his or her point of view. It's a simple way to find a like-minded Internet companion. You may even make a friend.

38

Chat with the Stars

We're waiting for Joni. I'm at home, sitting in front of my computer, with a cup of tea at my side and R.E.M.'s *Monster* on the stereo. Soon, the words of folk singer Joni Mitchell will be scrolling down my screen in an interactive interview. For now, there's not much to do but stare at a message from someone called OnlineHost—"Remember, your comments are seen only by other members of your row"—and chat with my "row-mates" in the online audience. I'm just one of hundreds of Netheads sitting in the rows of an "auditorium" and waiting for the event to begin.

"Is this happening?" I say. "Has it started yet?"

"Don't know," types TURBULENT1. "Maybe we're stuck in the last row."

"You mean we're way back in the blue seats?"

"You got it."

Finally, the folk star arrives, her name abbreviated to JoniMtchll, and off we go, with questions from the online audience about happiness ("it takes practice"), influences (Leonard Cohen and Bob Dylan), and the challenges of songwriting ("the music comes naturally...the words take polishing"). Once the questions begin, Mitchell gets into a groove, dispatching some of them swiftly, like the one about past loves, and spending more time on those that interest her.

Her thoughts on the author George Sand?

"I like the way she dressed."

What about pets?

"I have three cats," she says. "Pansy, Nietzche, and El Cafe."

Does she plan on writing a book?

"Yes!" Mitchell says. "I want to write several books, one a collection of short stories, another an illustrated book about my visits to Georgia O'Keeffe and Charles Mingus."

Mitchell is just one of the many celebrities who have appeared in cyberspace to answer questions in "real-time" events. Celebrities get to speak directly to fans in these interviews, avoiding the typical filters of the media, while fans have the chance for direct, if distant, contact with celebrities. Guests have included Woody Allen, Aerosmith, and Tom Clancy, among many others.

To attend one of these events, visit Chat Soup (**http://www.chatsoup.com**), a clearinghouse of celebrity appearances on the Net, and review the schedule of upcoming chats. Some events require you to be a member of a major online service, such as America Online or Prodigy, while others—like those at Barnes & Noble (**http://www. barnesandnoble.com**), Pathfinder Chat (**http://www. pathfinder.com/chat/**) and Talk.com (**http://www.talk. com**)—require only an Internet connection. The set-up varies from site to site, but often you're allowed to ask the guest questions and, at the same time, converse with a select number of audience members in a special "room" or "row."

Mitchell appeared on CyberTalk, a regular event on America Online. The "interactive talk show," as it's billed, usually lasts about an hour. Other CyberTalk guests have included Seal, Thomas Dolby, Laurie Anderson, and Slayer.

Netheads attend these events for a variety of reasons. Some come to quiz celebs and hear what they've got to say, while others just want to experience the novelty of participating in this unique, if developing and imperfect, medium.

One attendee of a cyber-appearance with Chris Robinson, the lead singer of the Black Crowes, said he dropped by the auditorium "to see what it was like." The verdict? "You can get a lot more out of this than reading an interview in a magazine," he said. "You get a chance to participate and maybe get in a question that an interviewer wouldn't ask."

A 17-year-old from a Washington, D.C., suburb, participated in an event with Biohazard, one of his favorite bands. He had a fun time, although he said it wasn't as "interactive" as you might think. "For one thing," he said, "when the artist answers your question, he moves on, giving you no chance to go in depth by replying to his response. Another thing is that there are so many people, it is often a disappointing experience, because your question never gets answered. Finally, when you put in your question it could be an hour before they get to it, if they do."

Still, he said he learned a lot about Biohazard. "Interacting with a celebrity is not like meeting them," he said, "but it is as close as many of us will get. Even if it isn't really 'live,' it is still exciting to see your name and question up on the screen knowing that everyone is reading it."

Of course, the question-and-answer format doesn't always lead to a discussion with much depth. In the Cyber-

Talk appearance with Robinson of the Black Crowes, the discussion had an unsatisfying, staccato feel to it. All Robinson wanted to do, it seemed, was cast off mildy witty one-liners.

"What do you do in spare time?" one person asked.

"Exist within the pressures of this modern world."

"What's with the hair on the CD cover?"

"It's growing."

And so on.

Despite the simplicity of the set-up, not everyone realizes they don't have a personal audience with the star. (A host generally screens the questions.) One person in my row at the Joni Mitchell event believed he was talking directly to her, one-on-one.

"I have really enjoyed listening to *Turbulent Indigo*," he said. "One of your best." Later, he asked, "Was there any specific event(s) that brought about 'The Magdalene Laundries'?"

"She can't hear you," said one of my row-mates, annoyed.

I explained the rules, and he left the row in shame.

Ah, the perils of cyberspace.

39

Dr. Internet

Of all the subjects on the Internet, health and medical information ranks among the most vast and varied, ranging from highly scientific papers to emotional testimonials from patients. Scattered in freewheeling discussion groups and across the far reaches of the Web, these resources haven't been packaged in a single, easy-to-read guide. Anyone looking for medical information on Net—even the experienced explorer of cyberspace—faces a daunting task.

Consider what happens when you enter the words **breast cancer** at AltaVista (**http://www.altavista. digital.com**), one of the Web's most popular search engines. The results? About 90,000 documents. One provides statistics on breast cancer in Hawaii, another discusses "a new DNA-based sequencing technique" and "p53 gene status," and another is a year-old article about the relationship between breast cancer and toxins from a student newspaper.

Handled properly, the Internet's medical information can lead to better medical care. But it can also lead to confusion and frustration.

To familiarize yourself with what's available on the Net, start with a visit to several of the most prominent—and reliable—online health sites. The top sites include the American Cancer Society (**http://www.cancer.org**), the American Heart Association (**http://www.amhrt.org**), the American Medical Association (**http://www.ama-assn.org**) and Healthfinder (**http://www.healthfinder.gov**). Internet Grateful Med (**http://igm.nlm.nih.gov**) provides access to the Medline database of journal articles from the National Library of Medicine.

If you're like most people who use the Web, you'll be able to spend hours exploring these sites—and following links to other sites. Don't worry about getting lost—sometimes that's productive (you never know what you'll turn up)—but be careful to evaluate what you're reading, watching out for peddlers of quick cures and anyone, in the words of one doctor, who's "a weird true believer in everything that's nutty."

Depending on what you're researching, you're likely to stray far from the site where you started. Maybe you began at the AMA site, soon found yourself at OncoLink (**http://www.oncolink.upenn.edu**)—one of the best cancer sites on the Web—and ended up at a Web page created by a woman whose father was diagnosed with cancer. Whatever route you take, you'll almost certainly find relevant—and helpful—material.

A general search of the Web, using one of the many search engines available, such as AltaVista, will likely turn up a lot more information than you want or need. (A search for retinoblastoma, a malignant tumor of the retina, found 1,000 documents.) It may take time to sift through these sites, trying to distinguish between what's reliable and what's not, but the search engines can be invaluable in locating information about the latest medical advances and the top specialists in a specific field. For rare disorders and less common conditions, a search of the Web can turn up an extraordinary amount of information—and it can do so in a way not possible just a few years ago.

After uncovering the Web's startling array of medical resources, you may start to wonder: "Isn't this my doctor's job?" It's a valid question, but you can't expect your doctor to know all the answers—or to have the time to explain the details of every available treatment option. A growing number of physicians see the Internet as promoting "patient empowerment" or "shared responsibility," with consumers taking a more active role in medical decision-making.

"Doctors will increasingly have a role as instructors, supporters, and coaches of self-provided care," says Dr. Tom Ferguson, author of *Health Online*. As for the peddlers of quick cures and other online hazards, Ferguson thinks that's more of a problem for newbies: "Sure, there's a lot of junk out there. It stands out like a sore thumb."

Internet-savvy consumers clearly have an edge in making health-care decisions. Those particularly adept at searching the Web and threading their way through discussion groups may be able to bring information to their doctors about the latest treatments available for a particular condition. Of course, patients should be careful in evaluating the credibility of the information they find on the Internet. Physicians spend years learning how to interpret medical literature. Be on the lookout for quacks and weirdos. Even when the advice is earnest, you should always make your decisions in consultation with a physician. Just because one person had a bad experience with a drug, or another touts a new procedure, doesn't mean it's for you.

40

Your Song

If you've ever argued about the garbled words to a rock song, you know it's not always easy finding an answer. The Net may be the place to look for one. Conduct a search of Yahoo! **(http://www.yahoo.com)** for **misunderstood lyrics**, and you'll find links to several Web pages with hilarious collections of lyrics people have mangled over the years, often causing them much embarrassment—and amusement.

At the Birdhouse Archive of Misheard Lyrics **(http://www.birdhouse.org/etc/misheard.htm)**, one person admitted to believing the line "Free free, set them free," from a Sting song, was "Free free, vasectomy." She discovered she was wrong when she was singing the song out loud with her boyfriend. After her boyfriend almost "killed himself laughing," he corrected her.

For whatever reason, a startling number of the misunderstood lyrics have to do with food. One person thought the Ramones song "I Wanna Be Sedated" was "I Want a Piece of Danish." Another thought the line " 'Cause you are the magnet and I am the steel," from the Walter Egan song "Magnet and Steel," was " 'Cause you are the mayonnaise and I am the steel." Yet another believed the line "I'll never be your beast of burden," from the Rolling Stones song "Beast of Burden," was "I'll never leave your pizza burning." Does listening to rock music induce hunger? Apparently so.

If you don't resolve your song dispute at one of the misunderstood lyrics pages, try one of the Web's search engines. A friend of mine once claimed there was a Billy Joel song with the line, "You make the rice, I make the gravy." Rice? Gravy? No way. I told him the line was "I may be right, you may be crazy," but he wouldn't believe me. A search of AltaVista (**http://www.altavista.digital. com**) for **+glass houses**—the title of a Billy Joel album— and **+lyrics** (see Chapter 10 for information on narrowing a search) yielded a Web page with the lyrics to the Joel album. The first song on the album was "You May Be Right." No mention of rice or gravy. The line was "I may be right, you may be crazy," as I thought. Argument resolved.

Another resource, the International Lyrics Server (**http://www.lyrics.ch**), allows you to search a database by artist, album and song. If you can't find an answer there, post a message to one of the **alt.music** or **rec.music** newsgroups. It's likely there's someone out there who knows where to find the specific lyrics you want, whether they were written by Cole Porter or Kurt Cobain.

41

Your Ancestors, Online

Forget *Myst*, and *Rebel Assault II*, and every other computer game you've ever played. You want a challenge? Start researching your family history, looking for the connections between your own life and the lives of ancestors from years past.

Genealogists see themselves as detectives, carefully assembling the pieces of their family histories. They scour county courthouses for records of births and deaths. They visit libraries and historical societies, leafing through the pages of old newspapers in the hope of uncovering details about ancestors they never knew. And increasingly, they turn to their personal computers—and the Internet—to assist them in their research and to organize the information they find.

For a genealogist, "You Don't Know Jack" is more likely to be the subject of an e-mail message about a great-great-grandfather than a computer game on CD-ROM. Who needs such games, they say, when you've got the labyrinthine complexities of genealogical research?

Constructing a family history does not require the use of a computer, but it makes the process a lot easier, mainly by connecting you with others who may have relevant information and by streamlining the process of maintaining a complex database of hundred of distant relations.

On the one hand, computers have become valuable tools for genealogists. Many cite the Internet, along with a favorite genealogy program, as essential to their work. On the other hand, the task of constructing a family history requires the genealogist to delve into the un-wired world of old photographs, letters, and other paper records. "Effective genealogy hunting requires long hours in libraries and archives going through old and dusty records, or writing letters to anyone willing to do the research for you," says Michael Cooley, owner of Genealogy Online (**http://www.genealogy.org**).

Yet the Internet, if used intelligently—without too much faith in its ability to provide quick and easy results—can help enormously in assembling an elaborate family history. "Before the Internet, genealogists had very few methods to communicate with others who were researching the same family lines," says Matthew Helm, publisher of the *Journal of Online Genealogy* (**http://www.online genealogy.com**). "Perhaps a few letters were exchanged after a genealogist found something in a library or heard of some information through a local society—a process that might take weeks or months. Now, genealogists can e-mail others halfway across the world and get an answer back in a matter of hours."

Others construct home pages with their genealogical research. Then, when someone else is researching the same surname, that person can make use of the information, or share additional material.

"The Internet allows people to conduct research and to communicate with others with minimal travel expenses and investment of time," says Helm. "The introduction of genealogical software packages and online research aids is making a tremendous impact on research and information organization."

To get started with genealogical research, begin with what you know, recording the birth dates of immediate relatives and the connections between them. Next, talk to older relatives (before it's too late, as genealogists often warn), being sure to ask to see photographs, old letters, birth and death certificates, family memorabilia, and other material with clues to your family history.

Once you have such basic information—and the sense that this is a hobby you'd like to pursue—consider your choices for genealogy software. The best of the commercially available genealogy programs, such as Family Tree Maker (**http://www.familytreemaker.com**) and Reunion (**http://www.leisterpro.com**), offer help in guiding you through the process of constructing a family history. A number of other programs, available as shareware, offer fewer features and less guidance, but often serve as adequate databases for your research.

Whatever program you choose, make sure it uses the standard file format known as GEDCOM (genealogical data communications). With the GEDCOM standard, you can exchange information with other genealogy programs— and with the people who use them. That's essential for genealogical research. You're likely to find others with information useful to you, and you want a program capable of importing that information.

Several years ago, genealogy programs served mainly as databases of family records, or "family group sheets," as genealogists call them. Now, they're capable of linking such data with photographs, audio interviews, and video clips. (Click on the photo of Grandma, and there she is, serving Thanksgiving dinner back in 1982.) Other features allow you to create lists of mailing addresses, birthdays, and anniversaries. Some programs even allow you to calculate life expectancies. As the sophistication of the software increases, the family trees constructed by genealogists will come to resemble multimedia extravaganzas, integrating written stories, home movies and dramatic readings of decades-old letters. Imagine Ken Burns's Civil War documentary, but about your own family.

Some genealogists publish their research on the Web, either to share with family members or exchange data with others researching related family lines. Of course, not everyone wants information about their families, some of it highly personal, available online. "In order respect the privacy of others," says Helm, "it's a good idea only to publish information about those who are deceased."

Once you have gathered the basic information available from family members, consider a trip to a local Family History Center. These centers, run by the Church of Jesus Christ of Latter-day Saints, have computers and other resources essential for serious genealogical research. (The Mormon Church is based on genealogy.) Next, visit one of the many Web sites with genealogical information. The best of these include Ancestry (**http://www.ancestry. com**), Genealogy Online (**http://www.genealogy.org**), Everton's Genealogical Helper (**http://www.everton. com**), the Genealogy Home Page (**http://www.genhome page.com**), the National Genealogical Society (**http://www. genealogy.org/~ngs**) and RootsWeb (**http://www.roots web.com**). The resources range from census data and marriage records to searchable databases of GEDCOM files.

Even with the help provided by genealogy programs and the Internet, don't expect to sign onto a Web site, type in your name, and download a reliable family history constructed by your father's great-uncle's grandson. In most instances, the government offices and organizations responsible for wills, obituaries, cemetery records, and county histories have not transcribed them—especially those from years past—for publication on the Internet. Alas, even with the latest high-tech tools, you may find yourself in the dark confines of a local historical society, learning about events from an era far removed from our own.

42

Of Neiman Marcus Cookies and Other Urban Legends

In 1982, when I was a sophomore in college, a friend of mine told me a story about a guy who'd gotten an "A" on a philosophy exam for handing in a blank test book. The question? "Define courage."

For 15 years, I believed that story. I told it to friends, and they told their friends. Now, I find out it's one of a host of "urban legends"—outlandish and oft-repeated tales, most of them false, passed from one dupe (like me) to another.

Peruse the stories at the AFU & Urban Legends Archive (**http://www.urbanlegends.com**)—home of the **alt.folklore.urban** (hence AFU) newsgroup—and you're likely to find one that you believed was true. Typical topics include "Alligators in Sewers," "Falling Cow Sinks Ship," and "Praying Mantis Laws." Urban legend aficionados revel in debunking "ULs," as they call them, and their banter can be rather amusing. To join the discussion of urban legends, or to contribute an urban legend of your own, visit

alt.folklore.urban, a Usenet discussion group "where nonsense is revered as an art form." Participants have a fun time mulling over the origins of ULs and pondering why people are so willing to believe them.

Despite all the debunking, the Internet probably does more to spread urban legends than to expose them. Post a wacky story to a popular forum, or send it by e-mail to a few friends, and soon it's got a life of its own, spreading across the Internet and undergoing a speedy transformation from truth to fiction. Consider the infamous story of the Neiman Marcus cookies. Over the years, various friends have forwarded me the same e-mail message from a man looking for "Internet justice." He claims to have requested a cookie recipe from a Neiman Marcus cafe, and when he was told the price, "two-fifty," asked that it be added to his tab. A month later, his credit card bill arrived, with the following line: "Cookie recipe—$250." Seeking "$250 worth of fun," he sent the recipe to all his friends, asking them to "post it anywhere and everywhere."

Of course, it's a hoax.

Visit the Neiman Marcus site (**http://www.neiman marcus.com**), and you'll find a "Cookie" link at the bottom of the page. "We have no idea who keeps spreading this rumor," Neiman Marcus says, "but we do know that it's absolutely untrue: We have no cookie recipe." Neiman Marcus shares its recipes for free.

Other sites for fans of urban legends include the Urban Legends Reference Pages (**http://www.snopes.com**), Legends from a Small Country (**http://www.web.co.za/ arthur/**), and Terry Chan's Main Urban Folklore Page (**http://www.nardis.com/~twchan/afu.html**).

Oh, and if there's anyone out there who knows the guy who got the "A" on that philosophy exam, please e-mail me. I'm still hoping it's true.

43

Buy, Buy, Buy

Whatever it is you're looking to buy, whether it's the week's groceries or a gift for your girlfriend, you're almost certain to find what you want on the Web. One online store sells caskets. Another sells chain mail. At Marie-Louise's Lucky Voodoo Boutique, you can pick up a "cosmic voodoo egg" specially designed to "help you enhance all areas of your life." The $9.95 egg comes complete with written instructions and a black velour pouch.

Not all of the Web's stores specialize in strangeness, of course. The best online outlets offer catalogues unrivaled by traditional retailers, along with the ability to enter the store anytime, anywhere. ("I can sit down at 2 a.m.," says one industry executive, "and order from my bedroom in boxer shorts.") Consider Amazon.com (**http://www. amazon.com**), an online bookstore with a catalogue of more than a million titles. Most mall bookstores carry only 30,000 titles, says Jeffrey Bezos, the company founder and CEO, while the largest bookstores have fewer than 200,000. A printed catalogue of Amazon.com's list would be the size of seven New York City telephone books. "When you have a large number of products like that," says Bezos, "that's when computers really start to shine." No wonder why Barnes & Noble decided to launch its own Web site, complete with online chats with authors, at **http://www. barnesandnoble.com**.

Anyone venturing into the world of cyber-shopping for the first time may be overwhelmed by the choices. The virtual world's storefronts vary wildly, with some sporting a glossy, highly produced look, along with access to enormous databases and elaborate ordering systems, while others offer only two or three items for sale and a message asking customers to send a check to a postal address or to call a phone number halfway across the country. At the Web's most reputable and popular retailers, the experience generally involves browsing for merchandise among selections of popular items or searching a large database of products. Many stores offer information not readily available at traditional outlets, such as product reviews, either from other customers or the press, and detailed technical specifications.

To bring an element of the familiar to the experience, many sites use the concept of "a shopping basket" to allow you to select items you're thinking about buying. Items can be added or removed from the shopping basket prior to checkout. Purchasing a product generally involves entering a credit card number, along with a mailing address, and pressing a button to submit the information. Many sites, but not all, use encryption to ensure the information is transferred securely over the Net.

The most sophisticated of the online stores attempt to turn their sites into much more than online catalogues. At CDnow (**http://cdnow.com**), a search for a specific artist—R.E.M., say—turns up albums, videos, T-shirts, and singles, along with a biography, a discussion group, photos and sound clips. It also directs you to the band's roots and influences (Big Star, the Clash, Patti Smith) and similar artists (10,000 Maniacs, the Feelies, the Replacements). At Reel.com (**http://www.reel.com**), where you can buy or rent movies, you can read reviews and ask for recommendations of movies similar to ones you've enjoyed. Even if you're not planning on buying anything, these sites can be a lot of fun for surfing.

And that, of course, is the idea: The Web's stores don't simply want you to visit when you're looking for something to buy. They want to provide a shopping experience, and they do that, most often, by providing information you can use, whether it's a review or a recipe.

44

Hot and Wired for the New Millennium

HotWired defines itself by what it isn't. It's not an online version of its print counterpart, the ultra-hip monthly *Wired*; it's not an online magazine "shoveled" into another medium; it's not an online service like America Online or Prodigy. "Like *Wired* before it," say the visionaries behind it, "HotWired is not a cold, marketing concept, but a heartfelt expression of the passion of its creators and its community—this community."

Okay, but what is it? Well, it's "New Thinking for a New Medium," or so they say, and it's one of the most compelling spots in cyberspace. To get there, point your Web browser to **http://www.hotwired.com/**.

A no-holds-barred blast into the digital future, HotWired covers politics, culture and technology with verve, author-ity, and a sometimes frightening degree of faith in all things tech. With its sub-sites, like Dream Jobs (with-it positions with cutting-edge companies) and Webmonkey (advice on everything from browser gadgets to low-res video), HotWired's gone further than any other site in crafting a brand identity for cyberspace. Sometimes the site's fun, sometimes it's frustrating, but it's always engaging.

Whatever you think of the site, it's clear the people who run HotWired have big plans for this new medium. They talk of the Digital Revolution, of the Second Renaissance, of integrating content with "a community space where users can interact with our staff, our contributors and each other." You'll find digital movies, serial dramas, off-the-wall art and lots of writing of interest to the cyber-savvy. In the spirit of community-building, HotWired includes a computer conferencing system for readers to contribute to the publication. "We're building something rich and strange here," says a message from the HotWired honchos. "Full of discussion, dialog, commentary, art, sound and vision. Help us define the future of this new medium." Go ahead! Do it!

45

....

Your Chat Companions

....

Imagine the doors to a thousand rooms, each tagged with names like Talk, Boogie, Albania, Losers, and Wunderbar. The doors list the number of people inside. You're not quite sure what's going on in any of these "chat" rooms, but you're free to enter—you don't even have to knock. Once you're in a room, you can listen to the various conversations—it's likely there will be more than one—and, if the moment's right, join in and start chatting. If it gets dull, you can leave one room for another.

That's what Internet Relay Chat **(irc)** is like—a bunch of rooms with people talking—except that in the realm of **irc**, you don't share a physical space, as at a cocktail party, but a mental one, with your companions sitting in front of their computers in places like Fearsville, Kentucky, and Canberra, Australia. For all they care, you could be typing in the nude or wearing your great-grandmother's wedding dress. They'd never know. **Irc** may not be as slick or simple as the Web's chat areas (see Chapter 3), but it remains one of the most popular ways to "talk" to others on the Net.

To get started with **irc**, you will need to install a new program on your PC. The most popular include Ircle for the Macintosh and mIRC for Windows. Ircle can be downloaded from **http://www.xs4all.nl/~ircle/**, while mIRC can be found at **http://pebbles.axi.net/mirc/**. (If you don't have luck with either of those sites, perform a search of Yahoo!—available at **http://www.yahoo.com**—for **irc**, Ircle or mIRC; that should lead you to sites with **irc** software to download.) The sites for Ircle and mIRC explain how to configure the software to begin using **irc**.

Once you have your **irc** program running, your computer will connect to another computer, known as a server, to provide access to the hundreds of **irc** "channels," as the chat rooms are called. Typically, you'll either be asked for a nickname or you'll be allocated one (you can change it later), and then, after a message with some network gibberish, you'll be ready to begin.

You can get by with a few basic commands. To execute **irc** commands, precede them with a /. First you'll want to ask for a list of channels, using the **/list** command. Typing **/list**, without qualifiers, will give you an unmanageably long list; instead, try **/list -min 7**, which tells **irc** to display channels with seven or more members:

```
/list -min 7
***Channel:  Users   Topic
*** #ny:      7
*** #polska:  17
*** #chat:    19      this used to be The
                      Friendly Channel <tm>
*** #happy:   8
*** #root:    23      weenies need not apply
```

Irc channels come and go, but a few, such as **#chat**, **#talk**, **#hottub**, **#england**, and **#sex**, have more devoted followings than others; they're usually up and running. Once you scroll through the list, you can enter a channel

with the **/join** command, using the form **/join** *#channel*.
Note that you must include the **#** sign that precedes all
channel names. To join the **#chat** channel, type:

```
/join #chat
*** Change: al9000 (ALLANHOFFM@bos1b.delphi.com)
has joined channel #chat

*** Topic on channel #chat is this used to be
The Friendly Channel <tm> #chat: al9000 bruc
fiver jewels Konrad igmokat firedog FuNgI
smartee Blaireau @Hecate nic @nAmes robert_
@Ames @Grimlaf _Nite_ @DEbot @Fedaykin @pfalken
```

You'll see a message, like the one above, confirming
your action, followed by a list of the people in the channel.

Now the fun begins. Anything you type, aside from
commands beginning with a **/**, will appear on the screens of
the other channel members. The name of the person
"speaking," in parentheses, precedes what he or she has to
say. As you can see from the following excerpt from the
#chat channel, a few groups may be carrying on conversations at once:

```
(igmokat) fiver!
(fiver) hi igmo
(bruc) hello?
(robert_) hey fiver!
(igmokat) >:|=
(firedog) Have you thought about having that
         looked at igmo?
(Blaireau) Konrad: Ach... du bist in polen...
(fiver) hi robert
(igmokat) firedog: what, my brain?
*** Change: bruc has left Channel #chat
(Konrad) Blaireau: Ausgezeichnet
```

```
(firedog) Igmo: Of course! :)
(igmokat) fire: nothing to look at ;)
```

It's a bit difficult to follow **irc** at first; you've got to get used to reading a few separate conversations as they scroll down your screen. In this one, bruc is saying, "Hello?" and then leaving. Meanwhile, igmokat, fiver, robert_, and firedog are greeting each other and discussing igmo's brain, or lack of one. And Blaireau and Konrad are talking in German.

As in other areas of the Net, a number of conventions guide the way people communicate with each other. When you direct your words to a specific person in **irc**, it's best to type that person's name, followed by a colon. Everyone will see the words, but the name and the colon will make it clear who they're meant for:

```
(igmokat) firedog: what, my brain?
```

On the other hand, you can send a private message using the **/msg** command:

```
/msg person's_nickname your_message
```

Whatever you type after the person's nickname will appear only on his or her screen. Let's say your nickname is vladimir, and you want to ask estragon a question:

/msg estragon What did we do yesterday?

Estragon will see the following on his screen:

```
*vladimir* What did we do yesterday?
```

It's best to respond to private messages with the **/msg** command. If you don't, your fellow chatters may think you're talking to yourself.

If you were allocated a random nickname, you may want to change it to something more suitable, using the **/nick** command. If your name was kent, but you want to be known as superman, type the following:

```
/nick superman
```

The following message will appear on your screen—and on everyone else's:

```
*** Change: kent is now known as superman
```

Anything you type will now appear from superman:

```
(superman) Anyone need help?
```

When you choose a nickname, think about what it reveals about yourself. If you're into in-line skating, try blade. Maybe you're a Frank Sinatra fan. How about nyny? Or would everyone think you're from the Big Apple? Hmmm... It's a tricky business, deciding on **irc** nicknames, especially when it comes down to gender. If you're a man, and you want to pose as a woman (or vice versa), just remember that channel members will see your e-mail address when you enter a channel. Then again, you're in **irc**, and pretty much anything goes.

If you're interested in learning about the members of a specific channel, use the **/who** command:

```
/who #channel
```

You'll get a list of the channel members' Internet addresses and nicknames. And if you want to learn more detailed information about a specific person, use the **/whois** command:

```
/whois nickname
```

If you want everyone to know about something you're doing, rather than saying, you're in luck. **Irc** allows you to express action, rather than speech. To express an action, use the **/me** command. Whatever follows the **/me** command will be broadcast as an action to your fellow channelites. Let's say your nickname is henry, and you type the following:

```
/me looks at the beautiful pond.
```

The following will appear on the channel:

```
*** Action: henry looks at the beautiful pond.
```

You can also express affection with the **/me** command:

```
*** Action: igmokat *schnoooooooooooozles*
    Hecate
*** Action: Hecate *huggles* igmokat
```

Or, more typically:

```
*** Action: firedog waves bye to everyone.
```

Aside from the ubiquitous "smileys" (see Chapter 19), you'll find that a lot of users favor brevity in irc:

```
(al9000) lucky u :)
(Skywalk) c ya later!
(lace) did u notice?
```

Here's a list of some of the most commonly used abbreviations on **irc**:

adn	any day now
bbl	be back later
bfn	bye for now

brb	be right back
btw	by the way
cul	see you later
fwiw	for what it's worth
<g>	grin
ga	go ahead
gmta	great minds think alike
imho	in my humble opinion
jic	just in case
lol	laughing out loud
oic	oh, I see
rotfl	rolling on the floor laughing
rtfm	read the f---ing manual
tnx	thanks
ttyl	talk to you later

To get help with **irc**, try **/help**; to leave a channel, type **/part** #*channel*; and to quit, use the **/bye** command.

46

In the Land of the
FurryMUCKers

If you want to cavort with furry animals in a virtual wonderland, **telnet** to **furry.org 8888**, the home of FurryMUCK, a thriving online community billed as "the first 100-percent anthropomorphic" MUD-like world. In FurryMUCK, don't expect to play a fantasy or sci-fi game with carefully defined rules, as you would in your typical MUD. MUCKs have a looser, more social atmosphere. At FurryMUCK, you can expect to join your fellow furries in building a virtual life with others who think it's cool to pretend they're furry and wild.

The characters on FurryMUCK have names like Pounce, Silkenfyr, and CoyoteLady. They talk to each other, toss things around and generally whoop it up. Sometimes they retreat to holes in the ground and have sex. If this interests you, type **connect guest guest** to enter the world of the FurryMUCKers.

To explore, ask for the help of a wizard, the furries who run the place. You can view a list of wizards by typing **wizzes**. Once you've got an active wizard's name, type **page** *wizard_name* = **I'm a guest, and I'd like to explore.**

Can you help me leave the Guest Room? (Be sure to include the = sign when paging someone.)

Wizards don't always cooperate, however, and you may have more luck, and certainly more power and freedom, by requesting your own character—though you may have to wait a day or two for your request to be processed. To acquire a character, decide on a name and check to see if it already exists by typing **page** *your_name_of_choice*. If the computer doesn't recognize the name, you're in luck—it's available. To get the character, disconnect from the MUCK—type **QUIT**, using all capital letters—and send e-mail to **join@muck.furry.org** with the character name and password you wish, along with the e-mail address where you can be reached.

Once you're admitted to FurryMUCK with your own character, **telnet** to the same address and connect by typing **connect** *character_name password*. You'll be dropped into a place called Under the Bandstand. It's a spot smelling of dusty leaves, with light streaming through the cracks in boards above you. You don't want to stay here long.

To leave, type **out**, causing you to "squirm out from under the bandstand, blinking in the sunlight." Once you're out from under the bandstand, you'll find yourself in the West Corner of the Park, a central meeting place on the MUCK. You'll notice a set of wooden folding chairs for furries to sit upon while listening to a band. You may hear your fellow MUCKers chatting:

```
A.J.Wolf sez, "I dunno, I love th'old Pogo
strip."
Strangeways states, "I'm partial to Fox Trot
myself."
RiffRaff purrs softly, "What's your favorite,
Tali?"
Snoopy growls, "Bumbazina and Albert became
Pogo."
```

```
Gozer walks over to Alex_bunny an Hi fives da
Puppet.
```

Unless you want to join the conversation, type **around** to get to a visitor's center for newcomers. Once there, type **read** to see what's on the bulletin board. To read the messages, type **read # (read 1, read 2,** etc.). These messages have information to get you started in your life as a furry being. If you feel like exploring, type **around** again, bringing you back to the West Corner of the Park, and then type a direction—**east, west,** what-ever—to head into the MUCK.

Once you've got your bearings, you should find a new "home" for yourself on FurryMUCK. By default, your current home is Under the Bandstand. If you continue to maintain your home there, the wizards will think you're a dormant furry and you'll be booted from FurryMUCK. For a new home, at least until you find a place you really like, type **@link me = #4498**; that will set your home to the Unicorn Inn, a temporary sleeping area. Typing **home** at any time will send you to the inn. If you want to change your home, type **@link me = here**, and your home will be changed to your current location.

Many of the commands on FurryMUCK resemble those at LambdaMOO (see Chapter 13). To say something, type **say**, followed by what you want to say. To move around, type a direction. Other useful commands include **look** (for a description of your location) and **look** *thing* (for a description of a room, character, or object). Type **get** *object* to pick up something. Type **drop** *object* to drop it. For further help with commands, type **help**.

You might also want to visit a Web site with information on the furry world. At the FurryMUCK WebStation (**http://www.furry.com/index.shtml**), you'll find everything you ever wanted to know about FurryMUCK. See you in MUCKland!

47

Gender Bending

The next time you spot a message in **alt.sex.wanted** from a man who describes himself as "dark, studly and willing to please the right babe," or a posting in **alt. personals** from a woman who says her "zoombas have been widely admired," you might want to question the individual's identity before you respond—that is, if it matters to you whether you're dealing with a he or a she.

No one knows how frequently the denizens of Netland "dress in drag," as it were—posing online as a member of the opposite gender—but there's no doubt it happens. For many, simply being on the Net means assuming another identity, one very different from their f2f (face to face) persona. A guy who's considered meek and shy offline, yet writes with wit, sarcasm and a lot of verve, can become an online celebrity in his newsgroup of choice, feared and admired by fellow posters.

Such a transformation—the possibility of it—draws newcomers to the Net. And if you can turn yourself from wimp into wizard, why not from a man into woman, and vice versa? Online, it can happen, and it does.

People have varying motivations for cross-gender posting, chatting, and MOOing. For some, it's a way to experiment, to give something a try, like wearing a wild and outlandish costume for a Halloween party—you take on another role for a few hours and see how you like it.

There's no doubt sex plays a big part in the phenomenon, with both men and women giving a go at attracting same-sex partners. And for women, propositioned one too many times in a newsgroup having nothing to do with sex or relationships (Do those dullards really think a woman visits **alt.atheism** to get a date?), a male identity may mean more respect and less "leering" in the testosterone-charged world of the Net.

If you want to try gender bending on the Net, give some thought to the place to do it and the risks involved. If someone finds you out, you may be in for some serious flaming, not to mention embarrassment. Start with an online gathering where it's tolerated, such as LambdaMOO (see Chapter 13). In LambdaMOO, a role-playing environment, you get to choose the gender of your character and build its identity. What's more, the genders aren't limited to male and female, making it a friendly spot for gender benders.

Posting to Usenet newsgroups is another option, but it's often difficult, if not impossible, to preserve your anonymity. In other words, bend your gender with care!

48

....

Searching by
Subject

....

Search for **mutual funds** at one of the Web's all-purpose search engines, and you're likely to end up with a page of "results" with unintelligible descriptions, like this one for a site labeled "Mutual Funds twentieth," whatever that means: "Mutual Funds twentieth Mutual Funds Prices for Twentieth Century Funds Feb 14, 1996 Mutual Fund Na."

Huh?

If you don't want to spend hours scouring an endless set of links, most of them described in gibberish, consider skipping a visit to the Web's general-interest search engines and trying one of the Web's subject-oriented search sites.

At Money$earch (**http://www.moneysearch.com**), one of the best of these, a search for **mutual funds** yields an orderly, easy-to-understand list of relevant sites, along with brief review of each of them. At the top you'll find INVESTools (**http://investools.com**), with the following description to give you a sense of whether it's for you: "Newsletters and research reports from 20+ top-name investment advisors. Stock picks and mutual fund ratings from impartial sources." That's a whole lot better than "Feb 14, 1996 Mutual Fund Na."

With so much material on the Web, and the amount growing each day, the generic search engines, such as AltaVista and Lycos, can sometimes be a morass of information, yielding thousands of links but little to differentiate what's valuable from what's not.

By contrast, Health Explorer (**http://www.health explorer.com**), with reviews of more than 3,000 health-related Web sites, offers brief descriptions of the sites, along with ratings—thumbs-up signs for the best sites—and a symbol to indicate whether the site is geared for health-care professionals. The site lets you search by keyword or browse among categories such as aging, disabilities, hospitals, mortality, and parenting.

At LawCrawler (**http://www.lawcrawler.com**), the categories include legal publishers, law reviews, and judicial decisions and case law, while WWWomen (**http://www.wwwomen.com**) includes categories such as women in business, diversity among women, feminism, and women's sports. The Yahoo! site for kids, Yahooligans (**http://www.yahooligans.com**), includes categories such as Art Soup (museums, dramas, etc.) and School Bell (programs, homework answers, and so forth). The site looks much like Yahoo!, but the listings have been pared down considerably. The movies section, for instance, includes sites for *Flipper* and *Toy Story*, but not ones for *A Clockwork Orange* and *Eraserhead.*

Other sites cater to even more specific audiences. MathSearch (**http://www.maths.usyd.edu.au:8000/Math Search.html**) limits the sites being searched to those concerned with "research-level and university mathematics." And AvatarSearch (**http://www.AvatarSearch.com**), billed as a search engine for occult information on the Internet, includes categories ranging from General Magick to Paganism and Wicca. A search for **witch** leads to a site for the Witches' League of Public Awareness (**http://www. CelticCrow.com**), "a proactive educational network dedicated to correcting misinformation about witches and witchcraft." It's not for everyone, but that's the idea behind this useful class of search sites.

49

....

Be an Expert

....

Inevitably, surfing the Net turns you into an expert on
the Net itself. After a while, you lose that sense of "Where
am I?" when you log on. Words such as **telnet** and **irc**
don't intimidate you. Things begin to make sense. Now,
when you see a reference to a MUD or a MOO, you think
of imagined-yet-real places, not wet dirt or the sound a cow
makes. All of this—the games, the sex talk, the art, those
billions of words and images—exists because of the almost
anarchic cooperation of people like yourself. The Net is not
burdened with bureaucracy and restrictive rules, yet it's
not brutish or unruly. For the most part, it's quite civilized.
It works.

In finding your way around the Net, you've probably
gotten help from a more seasoned Net traveler at one time
or another. That's the way of the Net, and now it's time for
you to share your newly acquired knowledge. You know
what you're doing, so help someone with less cybersavvy.

As you know from Chapters 3 and 4, chat rooms and
newsgroups can be some of the most freewheeling and

chaotic spots on the Net. They're also frequented by new-bies. Hang out in a chat room for more than 15 minutes, and you're bound to see a question about the Internet scroll down your screen. Maybe you'll come across one like this:

```
Anyone know how to build a home page? I've heard
about a few places that'll give you a home page
for free. You ever try any of these? Know
anything about them? I'd rather not learn HTML
if I can avoid it.
```

You can answer that one. (If you can't, read Chapter 7.) Perhaps you've even discovered some other sites offering free home pages. Share information about those, too.

Newbies need people like you. As new users come on-line, recently trained cyberjocks, those still with a sense of what it's like not to know the difference between **irc** and **telnet**, have to help them out. It's like settling the frontier. You learn the ways of the territory, you gain a feel for the lay of the land, and you help out the new arrivals. Such cooperation builds a sense of community and makes the Net a liveable place.

50

···

Explore!

···

The Net is a wild, untamed place—like the frontier—where outposts come and go, where explorers seek out thrills and adventure, and where one day's hottest destination seems dull and crowded a week later. If you've read and followed just a few chapters of this book, you've gained a sense of why so many people come away from their first experiences of the Internet feeling like they've seen another world; in fact, they have. "Awesome," they say. "Mind-blowing." "Way cool." Or, sitting in front of a computer, "Wow!"

Like most Net surfers, I revel in those "Wow!" experiences. You learn by exploring, and that spirit of exploration and discovery is at the heart of this book. If you find anything interesting—a weird game, an especially wild MUD, an impressive zine—write to me with the info.

I'm on the Net. You can find me at **alh@web100.com**.

Glossary

agent A program used to gather information from disparate locations and databases on the Internet, basing its selection of material on a user's personal preferences.

applet A mini-application, such as one created in the Java programming language and operated from a Web page.

application A task-oriented software program, such as those used for drawing and word processing.

ASCII (American Standard Code for Information Interchange) A computer industry standard for encoding the letters, numbers and other characters on a computer keyboard.

browser An application, such as Netscape Navigator or Microsoft Internet Explorer, for navigating the World Wide Web.

e-mail Messages sent electronically between computers.

FAQs (frequently asked questions) A document listing common questions and their answers, often posted to newsgroups and available via ftp.

GIF (Graphical Interchange Format) A common format used for storing and compressing graphic files.

host computer A computer that serves as a home base for users.

HTML (hypertext mark-up language) The coding system used to instruct a Web browser on how to display a Web page.

hypertext A nonlinear method for reading and looking at documents.

irc (Internet Relay Chat) A way for people to talk to each other over their computers in "real time" on the Internet.

Java A programming language used frequently in creating Internet applications.

K (kilobyte) The unit of measurement commonly used for files on computers; 1K equals 1,024 characters.

mailing list A way for people with similar interests to communicate with each other. A list of people subscribed to a mailing list is maintained on a central computer; any mail sent to the list address is routed to all subscribers.

modem A device to allow computers to communicate over telephone lines.

MUD (Multi-User Dungeon or Dimension) A "virtual world" in which a user takes on the identity of a character and participates in a role-playing game. Varieties of MUDs include MOOs, MUCKs and MUSHes. Some of these M-things emphasize social interaction over the competition prevalent in "traditional" MUDs.

newsgroup An electronic bulletin board with a specific focus, such as sex (alt.sex) or travel (rec.travel).

newsreader A program to allow you to read newsgroup postings, respond to messages and post your own items.

plug-in A program installed on a user's PC to work in tandem with the Web browser.

posting A message sent to a newsgroup.

push A method for transferring information to a user's PC. With push technology, material is delivered to a user's PC periodically, generally when the machine is idle or when the information is updated.

service provider A firm or organization offering access to the Internet.

shareware Software, often accessible online, made available on a trial basis by the programmer. If you decide to keep the software, you're asked to register your copy and pay a fee.

telnet A method for connecting your computer to another computer on the Internet. Telnet allows you to use the computer at your desk as if it were directly connected to the remote computer.

thread A string of related messages posted to a Usenet newsgroup.

Unix An operating system commonly used on computers connected to the Internet.

URL (Uniform Resource Locator) An address indicating where to find something on the Internet.

Usenet A collection of specialized electronic bulletin boards, known as newsgroups.

username The part of an e-mail address before the @ sign (the me in me@home.net).

World Wide Web A hypertextual area of the Net for browsing and gathering information.

Index

Addresses, 26-27
AfterShock, 120
Agents, 105-106, 181
Alt.personals, 85-88
AltaVista, 52-54, 79, 146-147, 150, 176
Amazon.com, 158-159
America Online, 12-13, 32, 82, 143-144
Ancestry, researching, 151-155
Applet, 29, 181
Application, 181
ASCII (American Standard Code for Information Interchange), 181
Auction houses, 99-100
AudioNet, 49-50
AutoWeb Interactive, 106
AvatarSearch, 176-177

BackWeb, 47
Barnes & Noble, 143, 159

Bartleby Library at Columbia University, 117
Beatrice's Web Guide, 95
BidFind, 100
BigBook, 78
Bigfoot, 78
BigYellow, 78
Bots, 105-106
BotSpot, 106
Browser, Web, 24-25, 29, 32, 181
Bulletin boards, 31-35

Castanet, 47
CDnow, 159
Celebrities
    chatting with, 142-145
    e-mail addresses, 89-90
Chat rooms, 28-30, 163-169
Chat Soup, 143
City guides, 128-129
City.Net, 129
CitySearch, 128-129

Classics, online, 116-117
CNET, 50
CompuServe, 13, 82
Computer Ethics Institute, 66
Connection to the
    Internet, 12-13
Cooperation, 178-179
Cyber-shopping, 158-160
CyberFiber, 82
Cybergrrl Webstation, 94
CyberTalk, 144-145

DejaNews, 79
Digital City, 129
Directory services, 76-80
Disinformation, 54-55
Diversity University, 69,
    102-104
Documents
    government, 135-137
    White House, 26

E-mail, 14, 140-141, 182
    celebrity addresses, 89-90
    signatures, 132-134
    White House system, 26-27,
        136-137
Electronic signature, 132-134
Emoticons, 91-93
Equipment needed, 12
Excite, 23-25, 55
Extreme Snowboarding, 118-119

Family history, researching,
    151-155
FAQ Finder, 84

FAQs (frequently asked
    questions), 83-84, 182
Flame, 61-64
Folklore, urban, 156-157
Four11, 78, 80, 89-90
Fully qualified domain
    name, 27
FurryMUCK, 170-172
FutureCulture, 36-38

Games, 68-75, 107-112,
    118-120, 170-172
GEDCOM (genealogical
    data communications),
    153-154
Gender bending, 173-174
Genealogy, researching,
    151-155
GeoCities, 43-44
GIF (Graphical Interchange
    Format), 182
Guide to Museums and
    Cultural Resources, 131

Hacker, 121-123
Haggle Online, 100
Health Explorer, 55, 176
Health sites, 146-148
Home page, 24
    building your, 43-44
Host computer, 182
HotBot, 55
HotWired, 141, 161-162
HTML (hypertext mark-up
    language), 43-44, 182
Hypertext, 24, 182

Information,
  sharing, 178-179
"Interactive Citizens'
  Handbook," 136
Interactive learning, 101-104
Interactivity, 140-141
Internet Address Finder, 78
Internet Auction List, 100
Internet Relay Chat
  (irc), 29, 163-169, 182
Internet, definition of, 11
INVESTools, 175

Jargon, 121-123
Jargon File, 121-122
Java, 29, 182
Journal of Online
  Genealogy, 152
Jumbo, 115
Just Sports for Women, 94

K (kilobyte), 182

LambdaMOO, 68-75, 102,
  172, 174
LawCrawler, 176
Letter writing, 140-141
Links, 24
Liszt, 38
Locating people on the
  Internet, 76-80
Love on the Internet, 85-88
Lurking, 31-35
Lycos, 79, 176
Lyrics-related
  resources, 149-150

Mailing lists, 36-38, 81-82, 182
Marimba, 47
MathSearch, 176
Mediadome, 50
Medical information, 146-148
Mello Smello Games &
  Coloring Books, 120
Metasearch, 56
Microsoft, 45-46
  Expedia, 105-106
  Internet Explorer, 24, 29
  Network, 13
Modem, 183
Money$earch, 56, 175
Monster Board, 106
MOOs (MUD Object
  Oriented), 68-75, 102-103
MUCKs, 170-172
Mudball Wall, 119
MUDs (Multi-User
  Dungeons), 68-69,
  107-109, 170, 183
Museums, electronic, 130-131
MUSHes, 68
My Excite Channel, 23-25
My Yahoo!, 23-25, 57

National Library of
  Medicine, 147
Neiman Marcus, 157
Netdictionary, 122
Netiquette, 65-67
NetLingo, 122
Netscape Navigator, 24, 29,
  32, 45-46
Networking, career, 81-82

Newsgroups, 31-35, 41, 79, 81-82, 84, 183
  book reviews, 139
  gender bending in, 173-174
  MUD, 109
  poetry, 138-139
  prose, 139
  sex, 85-88, 139
  travel, 124-127
  urban folklore, 156-157
  women's, 94-95
Newsreader, 32, 183

On-line Books Page, 117
OncoLink, 147
OnSale, 99-100

Pathfinder Chat, 143
PC Computing, 114
PC Week, 114
Playsite, 110-111
Plug-ins, 29, 48-51, 119, 183
Poetry newsgroups, 138-139
PointCast Network, 47
Posting, 31-35, 183
President, writing to, 26-27
Prodigy, 13, 143
Publishing, 138-139
Push technology, 14, 45-47, 183

Quatris, 119
Questions, frequently asked, 11-14, 83-84, 182

"Real-time" events, 142-145

RealPlayer, 49
Rec.travel newsgroups, 124-127
Reel.com, 160
Reunion, 153
RockyMud, 108
Rolling Stone, 140-141
RootsWeb, 154

Saturday!, 119
Search engines, 52, 54, 79, 175-177
Search.com, 56
Searching the Web, 52-57
Service provider, 183
Sex newsgroups, 85-88
Shareware, 40, 113-115, 183
Shockwave, 49, 119-120
Shopping, on the Internet, 158-160
Sidewalk, 128-129
Signature, electronic, 132-134
Smileys, 91-93
Software, 12, 113-115
Spamming, 72
Spoofing, 72
Stores, online, 158-160
Straight Dope, 97
'Stroids, 119
Switchboard, 76-80

Talk.com, 143
Teleporting, 72
Telnet, 39-40, 184
Thread, 184

Tile.Net, 82
Travel agents, 105-106
Travel newsgroups,
    124-127
Travelocity, 105
Tripod, 43-44
Trivia, researching, 96-98
Tunes.com, 51

UnfURLed, 54, 56
Unix, 184
"Urban legends," 156-157
URL (Uniform Resource
    Locator), 24-25, 184
Usenet, 31-33, 36, 41, 79, 184
Usenet FAQs, 84
Username, 27, 184

Virtual campus, 102-104
Virtual exhibits, 130-131
Virtual reality, 68-75,
    107-109, 170-172

WebFlyer, 106
WELL (Whole Earth
    'Lectronic Link), 39-42, 82

Whatis.com, 122
White House
    documents, 26
    e-mail system, 26-27
    online, 135-137
Whole Earth Catalog, 39
WhoWhere, 78
Wired, 140-141, 161
Women's issues, 94-95
Word, 51
Word Wizard, 97
World Wide Arts
    Resources, 131
World Wide Web, 14,
    23-25, 184
World Wide Web Artists
    Consortium, 81
Worldpages, 78

Yahoo!, 23-25, 29, 52, 54,
    57, 90, 129, 149, 164, 176
Yahooligans!, 54, 57, 176
"You Don't Know Jack,"
    110-112

ZDNet Software Library, 114